Randolfo, brothers to Albano
Quadratus
Laverdure, a Frenchman
Lampatho Doria
Simplicius Faber
Francisco, a perfumer
Philus, page to Jacomo
Bidet, page to Laverdure
Slip, page to Albano
Holofernes Pippo, page to Simplicius
A Schoolmaster
Battus, Nous, Nathaniel, and Slip, schoolboys
Noose, Trip, and Doit, pages
Celia, wife to Albano
Maletza, sister to Celia
Lyzabetta
Lucia, waiting-woman to Celia

INDUCTION

Before the music sounds for the Act, enter **ATTICUS**, **DORICUS**, and **PHILOMUSE**; they sit a good while on the stage before the candles are lighted, talking together, and on sudden **DORICUS** speaks.

[Enter **TIREMAN** with lights.

DORICUS
O fie, some lights! Sirs, fie! let there be no deeds of darkness done among us. Ay,—so, so, prithee, Tireman, set Signior Snuff a-fire: he's a choleric gentleman; he will take pepper in the nose instantly; fear not. 'Fore heaven, I wonder they tolerate him so near the stage.

PHILOMUSE
Faith, Doricus, thy brain boils; keel it, keel it, or all the fat's in the fire; in the name of Phœbus, what merry genius haunts thee to-day? Thy lips play with feathers.

DORICUS
Troth, they should pick straws before they should be idle.

ATTICUS
But why—but why dost thou wonder they dare suffer Snuff so near the stage?

DORICUS
O, well recall'd; marry, Sir Signior Snuff, Monsieur Mew, and Cavaliero Blirt, are three of the most-to-be-fear'd auditors that ever—

PHILOMUSE
Pish! for shame! stint thy idle chat.

DORICUS

Nay, dream whatsoe'er your fantasy swims on, Philomuse; I protest, in the love you have procured me to bear your friend the author, I am vehemently fearful this threefold halter of contempt that chokes the breath of wit, these aforesaid tria sunt omnia, knights of the mew, will sit heavy on the skirts of his scenes, if—

PHILOMUSE

If what? Believe it, Doricus, his spirit
Is higher blooded than to quake and pant
At the report of Scoff's artillery.
Shall he be crest-fall'n, if some looser brain,
In flux of wit uncivilly befilth
His slight composures? Shall his bosom faint,
If drunken Censure belch out sour breath
From Hatred's surfeit on his labour's front?
Nay, say some half a dozen rancorous breasts
Should plant themselves on purpose to discharge
Imposthum'd malice on his latest scene,
Shall his resolve be struck through with the blirt
Of a goose-breath? What imperfect-born,
What short-liv'd meteor, what cold-hearted snow
Would melt in dolour, cloud his mudded eyes,
Sink down his jaws, if that some juiceless husk,
Some boundless ignorance, should on sudden shoot
His gross-knobb'd burbolt with—"That's not so good;
Mew, blirt, ha, ha, light chaffy stuff!"
Why, gentle spirits, what loose-waving vane,
What anything, would thus be screw'd about
With each slight touch of odd phantasmatas?
No, let the feeble palsey'd lamer joints
Lean on opinion's crutches; let the—

DORICUS

Nay, nay, nay.
Heaven's my hope, I cannot smooth this strain;
Wit's death, I cannot. What a leprous humour
Breaks from rank swelling of these bubbling wits?
Now out upon't, I wonder what tight brain,
Wrung in this custom to maintain contempt
'Gainst common censure; to give stiff counter-buffs,
To crack rude scorn even on the very face
Of better audience. Slight, is't not odious?
Why, hark you, honest, honest Philomuse
(You that endeavour to endear our thoughts
To the composer's spirit), hold this firm:
Music and poetry were first approved
By common sense; and that which pleasèd most,

What You Will by John Marston

John Marston was born to John and Maria Marston née Guarsi, and baptised on October 7th, 1576 at Wardington, Oxfordshire.

Marston entered Brasenose College, Oxford in 1592 and earned his BA in 1594. By 1595, he was in London, living in the Middle Temple. His interests were in poetry and play writing, although his father's will of 1599 hopes that he would not further pursue such vanities.

His brief career in literature began with the fashionable genres of erotic epyllion and satire; erotic plays for boy actors to be performed before educated young men and members of the inns of court.

In 1598, he published 'The Metamorphosis of Pigmalion's Image and Certaine Satyres', a book of poetry. He also published 'The Scourge of Villanie', in 1598.

'Histriomastix' regarded as his first play was produced 1599. It's performance kicked off an episode in literary history known as the War of the Theatres; a literary feud between Marston, Jonson and Dekker that lasted until 1602.

However, the playwrights were later reconciled; Marston wrote a prefatory poem for Jonson's 'Sejanus' in 1605 and dedicated 'The Malcontent' to him.

Beyond this episode Marston's career continued to gather both strength, assets and followers. In 1603, he became a shareholder in the Children of Blackfriars company. He wrote and produced two plays with the company. The first was 'The Malcontent' in 1603, his most famous play. His second was 'The Dutch Courtesan', a satire on lust and hypocrisy, in 1604-5.

In 1605, he worked with George Chapman and Ben Jonson on 'Eastward Ho', a satire of popular taste and the vain imaginings of wealth to be found in the colony of Virginia.

Marston took the theatre world by surprise when he gave up writing plays in 1609 at the age of thirty-three. He sold his shares in the company of Blackfriars. His departure from the literary scene may have been because of further offence he gave to the king. The king suspended performances at Blackfriars and had Marston imprisoned.

On 24th September 1609 he was made a deacon and them a priest on 24th December 1609. In October 1616, Marston was assigned the living of Christchurch, Hampshire.

He died (accounts vary) on either the 24th or 25th June 1634 in London and was buried in the Middle Temple Church.

Index of Contents

STORY OF THE PLAY

Albano, a rich Venetian merchant, is reported to have been drowned at sea; whereupon his wife, Celia, is beset with suitors, and her choice falls upon a French knight, Laverdure. Jacomo, a disappointed suitor, plots with Albano's brothers, Andrea and Randolfo, to disturb the match, and for this purpose they disguise Francisco, a perfumer, in the habiliments of Albano; but the plot is detected by Laverdure's page, Bidet, who communicates the discovery to his master. The true Albano now arrives upon the scene, and encountering Laverdure, is accosted as Francisco, and is told that the plot has been discovered. Laverdure leaves him in a distraction of rage and amazement, which is not lessened when Jacomo and his own brothers approach and congratulate him on his powers of deception. A meeting between Albano and the disguised Francisco presently ensues. While Celia is entertaining her friends, Albano and Francisco clamour for admittance. Laverdure had told Celia (and the news had been spread abroad) that he intended to disguise a fiddler in the likeness of Albano as a foil to the disguised perfumer. When Albano and Francisco appear, Celia imagines that one is the fiddler and the other the perfumer. The true Albano and the counterfeit Albano, after engaging in a lively skirmish, declare that they will appeal to the Duke. When they retire Laverdure protests that he knows nothing of the new claimant, but his words are disregarded. The rivals appeal to the Duke, and the mystery is quickly solved when Albano, taking Celia aside, shows her a secret mark on his person, and reminds her of words that he had spoken on a certain memorable occasion.

DRAMATIS PERSONÆ
Duke of Venice
Albano, a merchant
Jacomo, in love with Celia
Andrea, and

Held most allowèd pass: know, rules of art
Were shaped to pleasure, not pleasure to your rules;
Think you, if that his scenes took stamp in mint
Of three or four deem'd most judicious,
It must enforce the world to current them,
That you must spit defiance on dislike?
Now, as I love the light, were I to pass
Through public verdict, I should fear my form,
Lest ought I offer'd were unsquared or warp'd.
The more we know, the more we want:
What Bayard bolder than the ignorant?
Believe me, Philomuse, i'faith thou must,
The best, best seal of wit is wit's distrust.

PHILOMUSE
Nay, gentle Doricus.

DORICUS
I'll hear no more of him; nay, and your friend the author, the composer, the What You Will, seems so fair in his own glass, so straight in his own measure, that he talks once of squinting critics, drunken censure, splay-footed opinion, juiceless husks, I ha' done with him, I ha' done with him.

PHILOMUSE
Pew, nay then—

DORICUS
As if any such unsanctified stuff could find a being 'mong these ingenuous breasts.

ATTICUS
Come, let pass, let pass; let's see what stuff must clothe our ears. What's the play's name?

PHILOMUSE
What You Will.

DORICUS
Is't comedy, tragedy, pastoral, moral, nocturnal, or history?

PHILOMUSE
Faith, perfectly neither, but even What You Will,—a slight toy, lightly composed, too swiftly finish'd, ill plotted, worse written, I fear me worst acted, and indeed What You Will.

DORICUS
Why, I like this vein well now.

ATTICUS
Come, we strain the spectators' patience in delaying their expected delights. Let's place ourselves within the curtains, for good faith the stage is so very little, we shall wrong the general eye else very much.

PHILOMUSE

If you'll stay but a little, I'll accompany you; I have engaged myself to the author to give a kind of inductive speech to his comedy.

ATTICUS

Away! you neglect yourself, a gentleman—

PHILOMUSE

Tut, I have vow'd it; I am double charged; go off as 'twill, I'll set fire to it.

DORICUS

I'll not stand it; may chance recoil, and be not stuffed with saltpetre: well, mark the report; mark the report.

PHILOMUSE

Nay, prithee stay; 'slid the female presence, the Genteletza, the women will put me out.

DORICUS

And they strive to put thee out, do thou endeavour to put them.

ATTICUS

In good faith, if they put thee out of countenance, put them out of patience, and hew their ears with hacking imperfect utterance.

DORICUS

Go, stand to it; show thyself a tall man of thy tongue; make an honest leg; put off thy cap with discreet carriage: and so we leave thee to the kind gentlemen and most respected auditors.

[Exeunt, all but **PHILOMUSE**.

PROLOGUS

Nor labours he the favour of the rude,
Nor offers sops unto the Stygian dog,
To force a silence in his viperous tongues;
Nor cares he to insinuate the grace
Of loath'd detraction, nor pursues the love
Of the nice critics of this squeamish age;
Nor strives he to bear up with every sail
Of floating censure; nor once dreads or cares
What envious hand his guiltless muse hath struck;
Sweet breath from tainted stomachs who can suck?
But to the fair proportion'd loves of wit,
To the just scale of even, paizèd thoughts;
To those that know the pangs of bringing forth
A perfect feature; to their gentle minds,

That can as soon slight of as find a blemish;
To those, as humbly low as to their feet,
I am obliged to bend—to those his muse
Makes solemn honour for their wish'd delight.
He vows industrious sweat shall pale his cheek,
But he'll gloss up sleek objects for their eyes;
For those he is asham'd his best's too bad.
A silly subject, too too simply clad,
Is all his present, all his ready pay
For many debts. Give further day.
I'll give a proverb,—Sufferance giveth ease:
So you may once be paid, we once may please.

[Exit.

THE SCENE:—Venice.

WHAT YOU WILL

ACT I

SCENE I

A Street.

[Enter **QUADRATUS**, **PHILUS** following him with a lute; a **PAGE** going before **QUADRUTUS** with a torch.

PHILOMUSE
O, I beseech you, sir, reclaim his wits;
My master's mad, stark mad, alas! for love.

QUADRATUS
For love? Nay, and he be not mad for hate,
'Tis amiable fortune. I tell thee, youth,
Right rare and geason. Strange? Mad for love!
O show me him; I'll give him reasons straight—
So forcible, so all invincible,
That it shall drag love out. Run mad for love?
What mortally exists, on which our hearts
Should be enamoured with such passion?
For love! Come, Philus; come, I'll change his fate;
Instead of love, I'll make him mad for hate.
But, troth, say what strain's his madness of?

PHILOMUSE

Fantastical.

QUADRATUS
Immure him; sconce him; barricado him in't,
Fantastical mad! thrice blessèd heart!
Why hark, good Philus (O that thy narrow sense
Could but contain me now!), all that exists,
Takes valuation from opinion,
A giddy minion now. Pish! thy taste is dull,
And canst not relish me. Come; where's Jacomo?

[Enter **JACOMO**, unbraced, and careless dressed.

PHILOMUSE
Look, where he comes. O map of boundless woe!

JACOMO
Yon gleam is day; darkness, sleep, and fear,
Dreams, and the ugly visions of the night,
Are beat to hell by the bright palm of light;
Now roams the swain, and whistles up the morn:
Deep silence breaks; all things start up with light,
Only my heart, that endless night and day,
Lies bed-rid, crippled by coy Celia.

QUADRATUS
There's a strain, law.
Nay, now I see he's mad most palpable;
He speaks like a player: ha! poetical.

JACOMO
The wanton spring lies dallying with the earth,
And pours fresh blood in her decayèd veins;
Look how the new-sapp'd branches are in child
With tender infants! how the sun draws out,
And shapes their moisture into thousand forms
Of sprouting buds! all things that show or breathe
Are now instaur'd, saving my wretched breast,
That is eternally congeal'd with ice
Of frozed despair. O Celia! coy, too nice!

QUADRATUS
Still, sans question, mad?

JACOMO
O where doth piety and pity rest?

QUADRATUS

Fetch cords; he's irrecoverable; mad, rank mad.
He calls for strange chimeras, fictions,
That have no being since the curse of death
Was thrown on man. Pity and piety,
Who'll deign converse with them? Alas! vain head,
Pity and piety are long since dead.

JACOMO
Ruin to chance, and all that strive to stand
Like swoll'n Colossus on her tottering base!
Fortune is blind—

QUADRATUS
You lie! you lie!
None but a madman would term fortune blind.
How can she see to wound desert so right,
Just in the speeding-place? to girt lewd brows
With honor'd wreath? Ha! Fortune blind? Away!
How can she, hood-wink'd, then so rightly see
To starve rich worth and glut iniquity?

JACOMO
O love!

QUADRATUS
Love! Hang love.
It is the abject outcast of the world.
Hate all things; hate the world, thyself, all men;
Hate knowledge; strive not to be over-wise:
It drew destruction into Paradise.
Hate honor, virtue; they are baits
That 'tice men's hopes to sadder fates.
Hate beauty: every ballad-monger
Can cry his idle foppish humour.
Hate riches: wealth's a flattering Jack;
Adores to face, mews 'hind thy back.
He that is poor is firmly sped;
He never shall be flatterèd.
All things are error, dirt and nothing,
Or pant with want, or gorged to loathing.
Love only hate, affect no higher
Than praise of Heaven, wine, a fire.
Suck up thy days in silent breath,
When their snuff's out, come Signior Death.
Now, sir, adieu, run mad and wilt;
The worst is this, my rhyme's but spilt.

JACOMO

Thy rhymes are spilt! who would not run rank mad,
To see a wandering Frenchman rival, nay,
Outstrip my suit? He kiss'd my Celia's cheek.

QUADRATUS
Why, man, I saw my dog even kiss thy Celia's lips.

JACOMO
To-morrow morn they go to wed.

QUADRATUS
Well then I know
Whither to-morrow night they go.

JACOMO
Say quick.

QUADRATUS
To bed.

JACOMO
I will invoke the Triple Hecate,
Make charms as potent as the breath of fate,
But I'll confound the match!

QUADRATUS
Nay, then, good day;
And you be conjuring once, I'll slink away.

[Exit **QUADRATUS**.

JACOMO
Boy, could not Orpheus make the stones to dance?

PHILOMUSE
Yes, sir.

JACOMO
By'r Lady, a sweet touch. Did he not bring Eurydice out of hell with his lute?

PHILOMUSE
So they say, sir.

JACOMO
And thou canst bring Celia's head out of the window with thy lute. Well, hazard thy breath. Look, sir, here's a ditty.
'Tis foully writ, slight wit, cross'd here and there,
But where thou find'st a blot, there fall a tear.

[The Song.
Fie! peace, peace, peace! it hath no passion in't.
O melt thy breath in fluent softer tunes,
That every note may seem to trickle down
Like sad distilling tears, and make—O God!
That I were but a poet, now t' express my thoughts,
Or a musician but to sing my thoughts,
Or anything but what I am.—Sing't o'er once more,
My grief's a boundless sea that hath no shore.

[He sings, and is answered; from above a willow garland is flung down, and the song ceaseth.

Is this my favour? Am I crown'd with scorn?
Then thus I manumit my slaved condition.
Celia, but hear me execrate thy love.
By Heaven, that once was conscious of my love;
By all that is, that knows my all was thine,
I will pursue with detestation;
Thwart with outstretchèd vehemence of hate,
Thy wishèd Hymen! I will craze my brain,
But I'll dissever all. Thy hopes unite:
What rage so violent as love turn'd spite!

[Enter **RANDOLFO** and **ANDREA**, with a supplication, reading.

RANDOLFO
Humbly complaining, kissing the hands of your excellence, your poor orators Randolfo and Andrea
beseecheth, forbidding of the dishonour'd match of their niece Celia, widow, to their brother—O 'twill
do; 'twill do; it cannot choose but do.

ANDREA
What should one say?—what should one do now? Umph!
If she do match with yon same wand'ring knight,
She's but undone; her estimation, wealth—

JACOMO
Nay, sir, her estimation's mounted up.
She shall be ladied and sweet-madam'd now.

RANDOLFO
Be ladied? Ha! ha! O, could she but recall
The honour'd port of her deceasèd love!
But think whose wife she was! God wot no knight's,
But one (that title off) was even a prince,
A Sultan Solyman. Thrice was he made,
In dangerous arms, Venice providetore.

ANDREA

He was a merchant; but so bounteous,
Valiant, wise, learned, all so absolute,
That naught was valued praiseful excellent,
But in it was he most praiseful excellent.

JACOMO

O, I shall ne'er forget how he went clothed.
He would maintain 't a base ill-usèd fashion
To bind a merchant to the sullen habit
Of precise black; chiefly in Venice state,
Where merchants gilt the top;
And therefore should you have him pass the bridge
Up the Rialto like a soldier
(As still he stood a potestate at sea).

RANDOLFO

In a black beaver felt, ash-colour plain,
A Florentine cloth-of-silver jerkin, sleeves
White satin cut on tinsel, then long stock.

JACOMO

French panes embroider'd, goldsmith's work, O God!
Methinks I see him now how he would walk;
With what a jolly presence he would pace
Round the Rialto. Well, he's soon forgot;
A straggling sir in his rich bed must sleep,
Which if I cannot cross I'll curse and weep.
Shall I be plain as truth? I love your sister:
My education, birth, and wealth deserves her.
I have no cross, no rub to stop my suit;
But Laverdure's a knight: that strikes all mute.

ANDREA

Ay, there's the devil, she must be ladied now.

JACOMO

O ill-nursed custom!
No sooner is the wealthy merchant dead,
His wife left great in fair possessions,
But giddy rumour grasps it 'twixt his teeth,
And shakes it 'bout our ears. Then thither flock
A rout of crazèd fortunes, whose crack'd states
Gape to be solder'd up by the rich mass
Of the deceased labours; and now and then
The troop of "I beseech," and "I protest,"
And "Believe it, sweet," is mix'd with two or three
Hopeful, well-stock'd, neat clothèd citizens.

RANDOLFO
But as we see the son of a divine
Seldom proves preacher, or a lawyer's son
Rarely a pleader (for they strive to run
A various fortune from their ancestors),
So 'tis right geason for the merchant's widow
To be the citizen's loved second spouse.

JACOMO
Variety of objects please us still;
One dish, though ne'er so cook'd, doth quickly fill,
When diverse cates the palate's sense delight,
And with fresh taste creates new appetite;
Therefore my widow she cashiers the blacks,
Forswears, turns off the furr'd-gowns, and surveys
The beadroll of her suitors, thinks and thinks,
And straight her questing thoughts springs up a knight;
Have after then amain, the game's a-foot,
The match clapp'd up; tut, 'tis the knight must do't!

RANDOLFO
Then must my pretty peat be fann'd and coach'd?

JACOMO
Muff'd, mask'd, and ladied, with "my more than most sweet madam!"
But how long doth this perfume of sweet madam last?
Faith, 'tis but a wash scent. My riotous sir
Begins to crack jests on his lady's front,
Touches her new-stamp'd gentry, takes a glut,
Keeps out, abandons home, and spends and spends,
Till stock be melted; then, sir, takes up here,
Takes up there, till nowhere ought is left.
Then for the Low Countries, hey for the French!
And so (to make up rhyme) good night, sweet wench.

RANDOLFO
By blessedness we'll stop this fatal lot.

JACOMO
But how? But how?

RANDOLFO
Why, stay, let's think a plot.

ANDREA
Was not Albano Beletzo honourable-rich?

RANDOLFO

Not peer'd in Venice, for birth, fortune, love.

ANDREA
Tis scarce three months since fortune gave him dead.

RANDOLFO
In the black fight in the Venetian gulf.

ANDREA
You hold a truth.

RANDOLFO
Now what a giglet is this Celia?

ANDREA
To match so sudden, so unworthily?

RANDOLFO
Why, she might have—

ANDREA
Who might not Celia have?
The passionate enamour'd Jacomo.

JACOMO
The passionate enamour'd Jacomo!

ANDREA
Of honour'd lineage, and not meanly rich.

RANDOLFO
The sprightful Piso; the great Florentine,
Aurelius Tuber.

ANDREA
And to leave these all,
And wed a wand'ring knight, Sir Laverdure,
A God knows what!

RANDOLFO
Brother, she shall not. Shall our blood be mongrell'd
With the corruption of a straggling French?

ANDREA
Saint Mark, she shall not.
She shall not, brother, by our father's soul.

RANDOLFO

Good day.

JACOMO
Wish me good day? It stands in idle stead;
My Celia's lost! all my good days are dead!

[The cornets sound a flourish.

Hark: Lorenzo Celso, the loose Venice Duke
Is going to bed; 'tis now a forward morn,
For he take rest. O strange transformèd sight,
When princes make night day, the day their night!

ANDREA
Come, we'll petition him.

JACOMO
Away! Away!
He scorns all plaints; makes jest of serious suit.

RANDOLFO
Fall out as 'twill, I am resolved to do't.

[The cornets sound.

[Enter the **DUKE** coupled with a **LADY**; two couples more with them, the **MEN** having tobacco-pipes in their hands, the **WOMEN** sit; they dance a round. The petition is delivered up by **RANDOLFO**; the **DUKE** lights his tobacco-pipe with it, and goes out dancing.

RANDOLFO
Saint Mark! Saint Mark!

JACOMO
Did not I tell you? lose no more rich time;
What can one get but mire from a swine?

ANDREA
Let's work a cross; we'll fame it all about
The Frenchman's gelded.

RANDOLFO
O that's absolute.

JACOMO
Fie on't! Away! She knows too well 'tis false.
I fear it too well. No, no, I have't will strongly do't.
Who knows Francisco Soranza?

RANDOLFO
Pish! pish! Why, what of him?

JACOMO
Is he not wondrous like your deceased kinsman, Albano?

ANDREA
Exceedingly; the strangest, nearly like
In voice, in gesture, face, in—

RANDOLFO
Nay, he hath Albano's imperfection too,
And stuts when he is vehemently moved.

JACOMO
Observe me, then; him would I have disguised,
Most perfect, like Albano; giving out,
Albano saved by swimming (as in faith
'Tis known he swome most strangely): rumour him
This morn arrived in Venice, here to lurk,
As having heard the forward nuptials;
T' observe his wife's most infamous lewd haste,
And to revenge—

RANDOLFO
I have't, I have't, I have't; 'twill be invincible.

JACOMO
By this means now some little time we catch
For better hopes, at least disturb the match.

ANDREA
I'll to Francisco.

RANDOLFO
Brother Adrian,
You have our brother's picture; shape him to it.

ANDREA
Precise in each point: tush, tush! fear it not.

RANDOLFO
Saint Mark then prosper once our hopeful plot!

JACOMO
Good souls, good day; I have not slept last night;
I'll take a nap: then pell-mell broach all spite.

[Exeunt.

Laverdure's lodging.

One knocks: **LAVERDURE** draws the curtains, sitting on his bed, apparelling himself; his trunk of apparel standing by him.

LAVERDURE
Ho! Bidet, lackey.

[Enter **BIDET**, with water and a towel.

BIDET
Signior.

LAVERDURE
See who knocks. Look, you boy; peruse their habits; return perfect notice. La la, ly ro!

[Exit **BIDET**, and returns presently.

BIDET
Quadratus.

LAVERDURE
Quadratus, mon Dieu, ma vie! I lay not at my lodging to-night. I'll not see him now, on my soul: he's in his old perpetuana suit. I am not within.

BIDET
He is fair, gallant, rich, neat as a bridegroom, fresh as a new-minted sixpence; with him Lampatho Doria, Simplicius Faber.

LAVERDURE
And in good clothes?

BIDET
Accoutred worthy a presence.

LAVERDURE
Uds so! my gold-wrought waistcoat and nightcap! Open my trunk: lay my richest suit on the top, my velvet slippers, cloth-of-gold gamashes: where are my cloth-of-silver hose? lay them—

BIDET

At pawn, sir.

LAVERDURE

No, sir; I do not bid you lay them at pawn, sir.

BIDET

No, sir, you need not, for they are there already.

LAVERDURE

Mor du, garzone! Set my richest gloves, garters, hats, just in the way of their eyes. So let them in; observe me with all duteous respect: let them in.

[Enter **QUADRATUS**, **LAMPATHO DORIA**, and **SIMPLICIUS FABER**.

QUADRATUS

Phœbus, Phœbe, sun, moon, and seven stars, make thee the dilling of fortune, my sweet Laverdure, my rich French blood. Ha, ye dear rogue, hast any pudding tobacco?

LAMPATHO

Good morrow, signor.

SIMPLICIUS

Monsieur Laverdure, do you see that gentleman? He goes but in black satin, as you see, but, by Helicon! he hath a cloth of tissue wit. He breaks a jest; ha, he'll rail against the court till the gallants—O God! he is very nectar; if you but sip of his love, you were immortal. I must needs make you known to him; I'll induce your love with dear regard. Signior Lampatho, here is a French gentleman, Monsieur Laverdure, a traveller, a beloved of Heaven, courts your acquaintance.

LAMPATHO

Sir, I protest I not only take distinct notice of your dear rarities of exterior presence, but also I protest I am most vehemently enamour'd, and very passionately dote on your inward adornments and liabilities of spirit! I protest I shall be proud to do you most obsequious vassalage.

QUADRATUS [Aside]

Is not this rare, now? Now, by Gorgon's head,
I gape, and am struck stiff in wonderment
At sight of these strange beasts. Yon chamlet youth,
Simplicius Faber, that hermaphrodite,
Party per pale, that bastard mongrel soul,
Is nought but admiration and applause
Of yon Lampatho Doria, a fusty cask,
Devote to mouldy customs of hoary eld;
Doth he but speak, "O tones of heaven itself!"
Doth he once write, "O Jesu admirable!"
Cries out Simplicius. Then Lampatho spits,
And says, "faith 'tis good." But, O, to mark yon thing
Sweat to unite acquaintance to his friend,

Labour his praises, and endear his worth
With titles all as formally trick'd forth
As the cap of a dedicatory epistle.
Then, sir, to view Lampatho: he protests,
Protests and vows such sudden heat of love,
That O 'twere warmth enough of mirth to dry
The stintless tears of old Heraclitus,—
Make Niobe to laugh!

LAMPATHO
I protest I shall be proud to give you proof I hold a most religious affiance with your love.

LAVERDURE
Nay, gentle signior.

LAMPATHO
Let me not live else. I protest I will strain my utmost sinews in strengthening your precious estimate; I protest I will do all rights in all good offices that friendship can touch, or amplest virtue deserve.

QUADRATUS
I protest, believe him not; I'll beg thee, Laverdure,
For a conceal'd idiot, if thou credit him;
He's a hyena, and with civet scent
Of perfumed words, draws to make a prey
For laughter of thy credit. O this hot crackling love,
That blazeth on an instant, flames me out
On the least puff of kindness, with "protest, protest!"
Catzo, I dread these hot protests, that press,
Come on so fast. No, no! away, away!
You are a common friend, or will betray.
Let me clip amity that's got with suit;
I hate this whorish love that's prostitute.

LAVERDURE
Horn on my tailor! could he not bring home
My satin taffeta or tissue suit,
But I must needs be cloth'd in woollen thus?
Bidet, what says he for my silver hose,
And primrose satin doublet? God's my life!
Gives he no more observance to my body?

LAMPATHO
O, in that last suit, gentle Laverdure,
Visit my lodging. By Apollo's front,
Do but inquire my name. O straight they'll say,
Lampatho suits himself in such a hose.

SIMPLICIUS

Mark that, Quadratus.

LAMPATHO
Consorts himself with such a doublet.

SIMPLICIUS
Good, good, good! O Jesu! admirable.

LAVERDURE
La la, ly ro, sir!

LAMPATHO
O Pallas! Quadratus, hark! hark! A most complete phantasma, a most ridiculous humour; prithee shoot him through and through with a jest; make him lie by the lee, thou basilisco of wit.

SIMPLICIUS
O Jesu! admirably well spoken; angelical tongue!

QUADRATUS
Gnathonical coxcomb!

LAMPATHO
Nay, prithee, fut, fear not, he's no edge-tool; you may jest with him.

SIMPLICIUS
No edge-tool. Oh!

QUADRATUS
Tones of heaven itself.

SIMPLICIUS
Tones of heaven itself.

QUADRATUS
By blessedness, I thought so.

LAMPATHO
Nay, when? when?

QUADRATUS
Why, thou pole-head! thou Janus! thou poltroon! thou protest! thou earwig that wrigglest into men's brains! thou dirty cur, that bemirest with thy fawning! thou—

LAMPATHO
Obscure me! or—

QUADRATUS

Signior Laverdure, by the heart of an honest man, this Jebusite—this, confusion to him! this worse than I dare to name—abuseth thee most incomprehensibly. Is this your protest of most obsequious vassalage? Protest to strain your utmost sum, your most—

LAMPATHO
So Phœbus warm my brain, I'll rhyme thee dead.
Look for the satire: if all the sour juice
Of a tart brain can souse thy estimate,
I'll pickle thee.

QUADRATUS
Ha! he mount Chirall on the wings of fame!
A horse! a horse! My kingdom for a horse!
Look thee, I speak play-scraps. Bidet, I'll down,
Sing, sing, or stay, we'll quaff, or anything.
Rivo, Saint Mark, let's talk as loose as air;
Unwind youth's colours, display ourselves,
So that yon envy-starvèd cur may yelp
And spend his chaps at our fantasticness.

SIMPLICIUS
O Lord, Quadratus!

QUADRATUS
Away, idolater! Why, you Don Kynsader!
Thou canker-eaten rusty cur! thou snaffle
To freer spirits!
Think'st thou, a libertine, an ungyved breast,
Scorns not the shackles of thy envious clogs?
You will traduce us unto public scorn?

LAMPATHO
By this hand I will.

QUADRATUS
A foutra for thy hand, thy heart, thy brain!
Thy hate, thy malice, envy, grinning spite!
Shall a free-born, that holds antipathy—

LAMPATHO
Antipathy!

QUADRATUS
Ay, antipathy, a native hate
Unto the curse of man, bare-pated servitude,
Quake at the frowns of a ragg'd satirist—
A scrubbing railer, whose coarse, harden'd fortune,
Grating his hide, galling his starvèd ribs,

Sits howling at desert's more battle fate—
Who out of dungeon of his black despairs,
Scowls at the fortune of the fairer merit.

LAVERDURE

Tut, via! Let all run glib and square.

QUADRATUS

Uds fut! He coggs and cheats your simpler thoughts,
My spleen's a-fire in the heat of hate;
I bear these gnats that hum about our ears,
And blister our credits in obscured shades.

LAVERDURE

Pewte bougra! La, la, la! Tit! Shaugh!
Shall I forbear to caper, sing, or vault?
To wear fresh clothes, or wear perfumèd sweets?
To trick my face, or glory in my fate?
T' abandon natural propensitudes?
My fancy's humour?—for a stiff jointed,
Tatter'd, nasty, taber-fac'd—Puh, la, la, ly ro!

QUADRATUS

Now, by thy lady's cheek, I honour thee,
My rich free blood. O my dear libertine!
I could suck the juice, the sirrup of thy lip,
For thy most generous thought!—my Elysium!

LAMPATHO

O, sir, you are so square, you scorn reproof.

QUADRATUS

No, sir; should discreet Mastigophoros,
Or the dear spirit acute Canaidus
(That Aretine, that most of me beloved,
Who in the rich esteem I prize his soul,
I term myself); should these once menace me,
Or curb my humours with well-govern'd check,
I should with most industrious regard,
Observe, abstain, and curb my skipping lightness;
But when an arrogant, odd, impudent,
A blushless forehead, only out of sense
Of his own wants, bawls in malignant questing
At others' means of waving gallantry,—
Pight foutra!

LAMPATHO

I rail at none, you well-squared signior.

QUADRATUS
I cannot tell; 'tis now grown fashion,
What's out of railing's out of fashion.
A man can scarce put on a tuck'd-up cap,
A button'd frizado suit, scarce eat good meat,
Anchovies, caviare, but he's satired
And term'd fantastical by the muddy spawn
Of slimy newts, when, troth, fantasticness—
That which the natural sophisters term
Phantasia incomplexa—is a function
Even of the bright immortal part of man.
It is the common pass, the sacred door,
Unto the privy chamber of the soul;
That barr'd, nought passeth past the baser court
Of outward sense; by it th' inamorate
Most lively thinks he sees the absent beauties
Of his loved mistress;
By it we shape a new creation
Of things as yet unborn; by it we feed
Our ravenous memory, our intention feast:
'Slid he that's not fantastical's a beast.

LAMPATHO
Most fantastical protection of fantasticness.

LAVERDURE
Faith, 'tis good.

QUADRATUS
So't be fantastical 'tis wit's lifeblood.

LAVERDURE
Come, signior, my legs are girt.

QUADRATUS
Fantastically?

LAVERDURE
After a special humour, a new cut.

QUADRATUS
Why, then, 'tis rare, 'tis excellent. Uds fut!
And I were to be hanged I would be choked
Fantastically. He can scarce be saved
That's not fantastical: I stand firm to it.

LAVERDURE

Nay, then, sweet sir, give reason. Come on: when?

QUADRATUS
'Tis hell to run in common base of men.

LAVERDURE
Has not run thyself out of breath, bully?

QUADRATUS
And I have not jaded thy ears more than I have tired my tongue, I could run discourse, put him out of his full pace.
I could pour speech till thou criedst ho! but troth,
I dread a glut; and I confess much love
To freer gentry, whose pert agile spirits
Is too much frost-bit, numb'd with ill-strain'd snibs,
Hath tenter-reach'd my speech. By Brutus' blood,
He is a turf that will be slave to man;
But he's a beast that dreads his mistress' fan.

LAVERDURE
Come, all mirth and solace, capers, healths, and whiffs;
To-morrow are my nuptials celebrate.
All friends, all friends!

LAMPATHO
I protest—

QUADRATUS
Nay, leave protests; pluck out your snarling fangs. When thou hast means, be fantastical and sociable.
Go to: here's my hand; and you want forty shillings, I am your Mecænas, though not atavis edite regibus.

LAMPATHO
Why, content, and I protest—

QUADRATUS
I'll no protest!

LAMPATHO
Well, and I do not leave these fopperies, do not lend me forty shillings, and there's my hand: I embrace you—love you—nay, adore thee; for by the juice of wormwood, thou hast a bitter brain!

QUADRATUS
You, Simplicius, wolt leave that staring fellow, Admiration, and adoration of thy acquaintance, wilt? A scorn! out; 'tis odious. Too eager a defence argues a strong opposition; and too vehement a praise draws a suspicion of others' worthy disparagement.
Set tapers to bright day, it ill befits;
Good wines can vent themselves, and not good wits?

SIMPLICIUS
Good truth, I love you; and with the grace of Heaven, I'll be very civil and—

QUADRATUS
Fantastical.

SIMPLICIUS
I'll be something; I have a conceal'd humour in me; and 'twere broach'd 'twould spurt i'faith.

QUADRATUS
Come then, Saint Mark, let's be as light as air,
As fresh and jocund as the breast of May.
I prithee, good French knight, good plump-cheek'd chub,
Run some French passage. Come, let's see thy vein—
Dances, scenes, and songs, royal entertain.

LAVERDURE
Petit lacque, page, page, Bidet, sing!
Give it the French jerk—quick, spart, lightly—ha!
Ha, here's a turn unto my Celia!

QUADRATUS
Stand stiff! ho, stand! take footing firm! stand sure!
For if thou fall before thy mistress
Thy manhood's damn'd. Stand firm! Ho! good! so, so!

[The Dance and Song.

LAVERDURE
Come, now, via, aloune, to Celia.

QUADRATUS
Stay, take an old rhyme first; though dry and lean,
'Twill serve to close the stomach of the scene.

LAVERDURE
This is thy humour to berhyme us still;
Never so slightly pleased, but out they fly.

QUADRATUS
They are mine own, no gleanèd poetry;
My fashion's known. Out, rhyme; take't as you list:
A fico for the sour-brow'd Zoilist!
Music, tobacco, sack, and sleep,
The tide of sorrow backward keep.
If thou art sad at others' fate,
Rivo, drink deep, give care the mate.
On us the end of time is come,

Fond fear of that we cannot shun;
Whilst quickest sense doth freshly last,
Clip time about, hug pleasure fast.
The sisters ravel out our twine,
He that knows little 's most divine.
Error deludes; who'll beat this hence,—
Naught's known but by exterior sense?
Let glory blazon others' deed,
My blood than breath craves better meed.
Let twattling fame cheat others' rest,
I am no dish for rumour's feast.
Let honour others' hope abuse,
I'll nothing have, so nought will lose.
I'll strive to be nor great nor small,
To live nor die; fate helmeth all.
When I can breathe no longer, then
Heaven take all: there put Amen.
How is't? how is't?

LAVERDURE
Faith, so, so; tellement, quellement;
As 't please opinion to current it.

QUADRATUS
Why, then, via! let's walk.

LAVERDURE
I must give notice to an odd pedant, as we pass, of my nuptials: I use him, for he is obscure, and shall marry us in private. I have many enemies, but secresy is the best evasion from envy.

QUADRATUS
Holds it to-morrow?

LAVERDURE
Ay firm, absolute.

LAMPATHO
I'll say amen if the priest be mute.

QUADRATUS
Epithalamiums will I sing, my chuck.
Go on—spend freely—out on dross, 'tis muck.

[Exeunt.

SCENE II

A School-room.

Enter a schoolmaster, **PEDANT**, draws the curtains behind, with **BATTUS**, **NOUS**, **SLIP**, **NATHANIEL**, and **HOLOFERNES PIPPO**, schoolboys, sitting, with books in their hands.

ALL
Salve, magister!

PEDANT
Salvete pueri, estote salvi, vos salvere exopto vobis salutem, Batte, mi fili, mi Batte!

BATTUS
Quid vis?

PEDANT
Stand forth: repeat your lesson without book.

BATTUS
A noun is the name of a thing that may be seen, felt, heard, or understood.

PEDANT
Good boy: on, on.

BATTUS
Of nouns some be substantives and some be substantives.

PEDANT
Adjectives.

BATTUS
Adjectives. A noun substantive either is proper to the thing that it betokeneth—

PEDANT
Well, to numbers.

BATTUS
In nouns be two numbers, the singular and the plural: the singular number speaketh of one, as lapis, a stone; the plural speaketh of more than one, as lapides, stones.

PEDANT
Good child. Now thou art past lapides, stones, proceed to the cases. Nous, say you next, Nous. Where's your lesson, Nous?

NOUS
I am in a verb, forsooth.

PEDANT

Say on, forsooth: say, say.

NOUS
A verb is a part of speech declined with mood and tense, and betokeneth doing, as amo, I love.

PEDANT
How many kind of verbs are there?

NOUS
Two; personal and impersonal.

PEDANT
Of verbs personals, how many kinds?

NOUS
Five; active, passive, neuter, deponent, and common. A verb active endeth in o, and betokeneth to do, as amo, I love; and by putting to r, it may be a passive, as amor, I am loved.

PEDANT
Very good, child. Now learn to know the deponent and common. Say you, Slip.

SLIP
Cedant arma togæ, concedat laurea linguæ.

PEDANT
What part of speech is lingua: inflecte, inflecte.

SLIP
Singulariter, nominativo hæc lingua.

PEDANT
Why is lingua the feminine gender?

SLIP
Forsooth because it is the feminine gender.

PEDANT
Ha, thou ass! thou dolt! idem per idem, mark it: lingua is declined with hæc, the feminine, because it is a household stuff, particularly belonging and most commonly resident under the roof of women's mouths. Come on, you Nathaniel, say you, say you next; not too fast; say tretably: say.

NATHANIEL
Mascula dicuntur monosyllaba nomina quædam.

PEDANT
Faster! faster!

NATHANIEL

Ut sal, sol, ren et splen: car, ser, vir, vas, vadis, as, mas,
Bes, cres, pres et pes, glis, glirens habens genetivo,
Mos, flos, ros et tros, muns, dens, mons, pons—

PEDANT
Rup, tup, snup, slup, bor, hor, cor, mor. Holla! holla! holla! you Holofernes Pippo, put him down. Wipe your nose: fie, on your sleeve! where's your muckender your grandmother gave you? Well, say on; say on.

HOLOFERNES
Pree, master, what word's this?

PEDANT
Ass! ass!

HOLOFERNES
As in presenti perfectum format in, in, in—

PEDANT
In what, sir?

HOLOFERNES
Perfectum format. In what, sir?

PEDANT
In what, sir?—in avi.

HOLOFERNES
In what, sir?—in avi.
Ut no, nas, navi, vocito, vocitas, voci, voci, voci—

PEDANT
What's next?

HOLOFERNES
Voci—what's next?

PEDANT
Why, thou ungracious child! thou simple animal! thou barnacle! Nous,—snare him; take him up: and you were my father, you should up.

HOLOFERNES
Indeed I am not your father. O Lord! now, for God sake, let me go out. My mother told a thing: I shall bewray all else. Hark, you, master: my grandmother entreats you to come to dinner to-morrow morning,

PEDANT
I say, untruss—take him up. Nous, despatch! what, not perfect in an as in presenti?

HOLOFERNES
In truth I'll be as perfect an as in presenti as any of this company, with the grace of God, law: this once—this once—and I do so any more—

PEDANT
I say, hold him up!

HOLOFERNES
Ha, let me say my prayers first. You know not what you ha' done now; all the syrup of my brain is run into my buttocks, and ye spill the juice of my wit well. Ha, sweet! ha, sweet! honey, Barbary sugar, sweet master.

PEDANT
Sans tricks, trifles, delays, demurrers, procrastinations, or retardations, mount him, mount him.

[Enter **QUADRATUS**, **LAMPATHO**, **LAVERDURE**, and **SIMPLICIUS**.

QUADRATUS
Be merciful, my gentle signior.

LAVERDURE
We'll sue his pardon out.

PEDANT
He is reprieved: and now, Apollo bless your brains; facundius, and elaborate elegance make your presence gracious in the eyes of your mistress.

LAVERDURE
You must along with us; lend private ear.

SIMPLICIUS
What is your name?

HOLOFERNES
Holofernes Pippo.

SIMPLICIUS
Who gave you that name? Nay, let me alone for sposing of a scholar.

HOLOFERNES
My godfathers and godmothers in my baptism.

SIMPLICIUS
Truly, gallants, I am enamoured on thee, boy; wilt thou serve me?

HOLOFERNES
Yes, and please my grandmother, when I come to years of discretion.

PEDANT
And you have a propensitude to him, he shall be for you. I was solicited to grant him leave to play the lady in comedies presented by children; but I knew his voice was too small, and his stature too low. Sing, sing a treble, Holofernes: sing.
[The Song.
A very small sweet voice, I'll assure you.

QUADRATUS
'Tis smally sweet indeed.

SIMPLICIUS
A very pretty child. Hold up thy head. There; buy thee some plums.

QUADRATUS
Nay, they must play; you go along with us.

PEDANT
Ludendi venia est petita et concessa.

ALL
Gratias.

SIMPLICIUS
Pippo's my page. How like you him? Ha! has he not a good face, ha?

LAVERDURE
Exceedingly amiable. Come away;
I long to see my love, my Celia.

SIMPLICIUS
Carry my rapier; hold up so; good child: stay, gallants. Umph! a sweet face.

[Exeunt all but **LAMPATHO** and **QUADRATUS**.

LAMPATHO
I relish not this mirth; my spirit is untwist;
My heart is ravell'd out in discontents.
I am deep-thoughtful, and I shoot my soul
Through all creation of omnipotence.

QUADRATUS
What, art melancholy, Lamp? I'll feed thy humour:
I'll give thee reason strait to hang thyself.
Mark't, mark't: in Heaven's handiwork there's naught—
Believe it.

LAMPATHO
In Heaven's handiwork there's naught,

None more vile, accursed, reprobate to bliss,
Than man; and 'mong men a scholar most.
Things only fleshly sensitive, an ox or horse,
They live and eat, and sleep, and drink, and die,
And are not touched with recollections
Of things o'er-past, or stagger'd infant doubts
Of things succeeding; but leave the manly beasts,
And give but pence apiece to have a sight
Of beastly man now—

SIMPLICIUS [From within]
What so, Lampatho! Good truth, I will not pay your ordinary if you come not.

LAMPATHO
Dost thou hear that voice? I'll make a parrot now
As good a man as he in fourteen nights.
I never heard him vent a syllable
Of his own creating since I knew the use
Of eyes and ears. Well, he's perfect blest,
Because a perfect beast. I'll gage my heart
He knows no difference essential
'Twixt my dog and him. The whoreson sot is blest,
Is rich in ignorance, makes fair usance on't,
And every day augments his barbarism.
So love me calmness, I do envy him for't.
I was a scholar: seven useful springs
Did I deflower in quotations
Of cross'd opinions 'bout the soul of man.
The more I learnt the more I learnt to doubt:
Knowledge and wit, faith's foes, turn faith about.

SIMPLICIUS [From within]
Nay, come, good signior. I stay all the gentlemen here. I would fain give my pretty page a pudding-pie.

LAMPATHO
Honest epicure.—Nay, mark, list. Delight,
Delight, my spaniel slept, whilst I baus'd leaves,
Toss'd o'er the dunces, pored on the old print
Of titled words, and still my spaniel slept.
Whilst I wasted lamp-oil, bated my flesh,
Shrunk up my veins; and still my spaniel slept.
And still I held converse with Zabarell,
Aquinas, Scotus, and the musty saw
Of antic Donate; still my spaniel slept
Still went on went I; first an sit anima,
Then, and it were mortal. O hold, hold! at that
They're at brain-buffets, fell by the ears amain
Pell-mell together; still my spaniel slept.

Then whether 'twere corporeal, local, fix'd,
Extraduce; but whether 't had free will
Or no, ho philosophers
Stood banding factions all so strongly propp'd,
I stagger'd, knew not which was firmer part;
But thought, quoted, read, observ'd, and pried,
Stuff'd noting-books; and still my spaniel slept.
At length he waked and yawn'd and by yon sky,
For aught I know he knew as much as I.

SIMPLICIUS [From within]
Delicate good Lampatho, come away. I assure you I'll give but twopence more.

LAMPATHO
How 'twas created, how the soul exists:
One talks of motes, the soul was made of motes;
Another fire, t'other light, a third
A spark of star-like nature;
Hippo water, Anaximenes air,
Aristoxenus music; Critias, I know not what.
A company of odd phrenetici!
Did eat my youth; and when I crept abroad,
Finding my numbness in this nimble age,
I fell a-railing; but now, soft and slow,
I know I know naught but I naught do know.
What shall I do—what plot, what course pursue?

QUADRATUS
Why, turn a temporist, row with the tide,
Pursue the cut, the fashion of the age.
Well, here's my scholar's course: first get a school,
And then a ten-pound cure; keep both. Then buy
(Stay, marry, ay, marry) then a farm, or so:
Serve God and mammon—to the devil go.
Affect some sect—ay, 'tis the sect is it,
So thou canst seem, 'tis held the precious wit.
And O, if thou canst get some higher seat,
Where thou mayest sell your holy portion
(Which charitable Providence ordained,
In sacred bounty, for a blessèd use),
Alien the glebe, entail it to thy loins,
Entomb it in thy grave,
Past resurrection to his native use!
Now, if there be a hell, and such swine saved,
Heaven take all—that's all my hopes have craved.

[Enter **PIPPO**.

PIPPO
My Simplicias master—

LAMPATHO
Your master Simplicius.

PIPPO
Has come to you to sent—

LAMPATHO
Has sent to me to come.

PIPPO
Ha! ha! has bought me a fine dagger, and a hat and a feather! I can say As in presenti now!
Company of Boys within. Quadratus, Quadratus, away! away!

QUADRATUS
We come, sweet gallants; and grumbling hate lie still,
And turn fantastic! He that climbs a hill
Must wheel about; the ladder to account
Is sly dissemblance: he that means to mount
Must lie all level in the prospective
Of eager-sighted greatness. Thou wouldst thrive:
The Venice state is young, loose, and unknit,
Can relish naught but luscious vanities.
Go, fit his tooth. O glavering flattery!
How potent art thou! Front, look brisk and sleek.—
That such base dirt as you should dare to reek
In princes' nostrils!—Well, my scene is long.

ALL [Within]
Quadratus!

QUADRATUS
I come, hot bloods. Those that their state would swell,
Must bear a counter-face. The devil and hell
Confound them all! That's all my prayers exact:
So ends our chat;—sound music for the act!

[Exeunt.

ACT III

SCENE I

Francisco's house.

Enter **FRANCISCO**, half-dressed, in his black doublet and round cap, the rest rich; Jacomo bearing his hat and feather; Andrea his doublet and band; Randolfo his cloak and staff. They clothe Francisco whilst Bidet creeps in and observes them. Much of this done whilst the Act is playing.

FRANCISCO
For God's sake, remember to take special marks of me, or you will ne'er be able to know me.

ANDREA
Why, man?

FRANCISCO
Why, good faith, I scarce know myself; already me thinks I should remember to forget myself; now I am so shining brave. Indeed Francisco was always a sweet youth, for I am a perfumer; but thus brave! I am an alien to it. Would you make me like the drown'd Albano? Must I bear't mainly up? Must I be he?

RANDOLFO
What else, man? O, what else?

JACOMO
I warrant you, give him but fair rich clothes,
He can be ta'en, reputed anything.
Apparel's grown a god, and goes more neat;
Makes men of rags, which straight he bears aloft,
Like patch'd-up scarecrows to affright the rout
Of the idolatrous vulgar that worship images,
Stand awed and bare-scalp'd at the gloss of silks,
Which, like the glorious A-jax of Lincoln's-Inn
(Survey'd with wonder by me when I lay
Factor in London), laps up naught but filth
And excrements, that bear the shape of men,
Whose inside every daw would peck and tear,
But that vain scarecrow clothes entreats forbear.

FRANCISCO
You would have me take upon me, Albano,
A valiant gallant Venetian burgomasco.
Well my beard, my feather, short sword, and my oath,
Shall do't, fear not. What! I know a number,
By the sole warrant of a lappy beard,
A rain-beat plume, and a good chop-filling oath,
With an odd French shrug, and "by the Lord," or so,
Ha' leapt into sweet captain with such ease
As you would—Fear't not. I'll gage my heart I'll do't.
How sits my hat? Ha! Jack, doth my feather wag?

JACOMO
Methinks now, in the common sense of fashion,

Thou shouldst grow proud, and like a fore-horse view,
None but beforehand gallants; as for sides,
Study a faint salute, give a strange eye;
And those that rank in equal file with thee,
But as to those in rearward, O be blind!
The world wants eyes—it cannot see behind.

FRANCISCO
Where is the strumpet? Where's the hot-vein'd French?
Lives not Albano? Hath Celia so forgot
Albano's love, that she must forthwith wed
A runabout, a skipping Frenchman?

JACOMO
Now you must grow in heat, and stut.

FRANCISCO
An odd phantasma—a beggar—a sir—a who, who, who—What You Will—a straggling go-go-go-gunds—
f-f-f-f-fut—

ANDREA
Passing like him—passing like him. O 'twill strike all dead!

RANDOLFO
I am ravished! 'Twill be peerless exquisite
Let him go out instantly!

JACOMO
O, not till twilight; meantime I'll prop up
The tottering rumour of Albano's scape,
And safe arrival; it begins to spread.
If this plot live, Frenchman, thy hopes are dead.

[Exeunt.

BIDET
And if it live, strike off this little head.

[Exit.

SCENE II

A Public Place.

Enter **ALBANO** with **SLIP**, his Page.

ALBANO

Can it be? Is't possible? Is't within the bounds of faith? O villainy!

SLIP

The clapper of rumour strikes on both sides, ringing out the French knight is in firm possession of my mistress, your wife.

ALBANO

Is't possible I should be dead so soon In her affects? How long is't since our shipwrack?

SLIP

Faith, I have little arithmetic in me, yet I remember the storm made me cast up perfectly the whole sum of all I had receiv'd; three days before I was liquor'd soundly; my guts were rinced 'fore the heavens. I look as pale ever since, as if I had ta'en the diet this spring.

ALBANO

But how long is't since our shipwrack?

SLIP

Marry, since we were hung by the heels on the batch of Sicily, to make a jail-delivery of the sea in our maws, 'tis just three months. Shall I speak like a poet?—thrice hath the horned moon—

ALBANO

Talk not of horns. O Celia! How oft,
When thou hast laid thy cheek upon my breast,
And with lascivious petulancy sued
For hymeneal dalliance, marriage-rites;—
O then, how oft, with passionate protests
And zealous vows, hast thou obliged thy love,
In dateless bands, unto Albano's breast!
Then, did I but mention second marriage,
With what a bitter hate would she inveigh
'Gainst retail'd wedlocks! "O!" would she lisp,
"If you should die,"—then would she slide a tear,
And with a wanton languishment intwist
Her hands,—"O God, and you should die! Marry?
Could I love life, my dear Albano dead?
Should any prince possess his widow's bed?"
And now, see, see, I am but rumour'd drown'd.

SLIP

She'll make you prince;—your worship must be crown'd.
O master, you know the woman is the weaker creature!
She must have a prop. The maid is the brittle metal;
Her head is quickly crack'd. The wife is queasy-stomach'd,
She must be fed with novelties. But, then, what's your widow?
Custom is a second nature;—I say no more, but think you the rest.

ALBANO
If love be holy; if that mystery
Of co-united hearts be sacrament;
If the unbounded goodness have infused
A sacred ardour, if a mutual love,
Into our species, of those amorous joys,
Those sweets of life, those comforts even in death,
Spring from a cause above our reason's reach;—
If that clear flame deduce his heat from heaven;—
'Tis like his cause, eternal, always One,
As is th' instiller of divinest love,
Unchanged by time, immortal maugre death!
But O, 'tis grown a figment, love a jest,
A comic poesy! The soul of man is rotten,
Even to the core;—no sound affection.
Our love is hollow-vaulted—stands on props
Of circumstance, profit, or ambitious hopes!
The other tissue gown, or chain of pearl,
Makes my coy minx to nuzzel 'twixt the breasts
Of her lull'd husband; t'other carkanet
Deflowers that lady's bed. One hundred more
Marries that loathèd blowze;—one ten-pound odds,
In promised jointure, makes the hard-palm'd sire
Enforce his daughter's tender lips to start
At the sharp touch of some loath'd stubbèd beard;
The first pure time, the golden age, is fled.
Heaven knows I lie,—'tis now the age of gold,—
For it all marreth, and even virtue's sold!

SLIP
Master, will you trust me, and I'll—

ALBANO
Yes, boy, I'll trust thee. Babes and fools I'll trust;
But servants' faith, wives' love, or female's lust,—
A usurer and the devil sooner. Now, were I dead,
Methinks I see a huff-cap swaggering sir
Pawning my plate, my jewels mortgage; nay,
Selling outright the purchase of my brows,
Whilst my poor fatherless, lean, totter'd son—
My gentry's relics, my house's only prop—
Is saw'd asunder, lies forlorn, all bleak
Unto the griefs of sharp necessities,
Whilst his father-in-law, his father-in-devil, or d-d-d-d-devil-f-f-f-father,
Or who, who, who, who,—What You Will!—
When is the marriage morn?

SLIP

Even next rising sun.

ALBANO
Good, good, good! Go to my brother Andrea:
Tell him I'll lurk; stay, tell him I'll lurk: stay.—
Now is Albano's marriage-bed new hung
With fresh rich curtains! Now are my valence up,
Emboss'd with orient pearl, my grandsire's gift!
Now are the lawn sheets fumed with violets,
To fresh the pall'd lascivious appetite!
Now work the cooks, the pastry sweats with slaves;
The march-panes glitter: now, now, the musicians
Hover with nimble sticks o'er squeaking crowds,
Tickling the dried guts of a mewing cat.

The tailors, starchers, sempsters, butchers, poulterers, mercers,—all, all, all,—now, now, now,—none think o' me,—the f-f-f-French is te f-f-f-fine man, de p-p-p-pock man, de—

SLIP
Peace, peace! stand conceal'd. Yonder, by all descriptions, is he would be husband of my mistress;—your wife! hah, meat, hah!

ALBANO
Uds so, so, so soul! that's my velvet cloak!

SLIP
O peace! observe him: ha!

[Enter **LAVERDURE** and **BIDET**, talking; **QUADRATUS**, **LAMPATHO**, **SIMPLICIUS**, **PEDANT**, and **HOLOFERNES PIPPO**.

BIDET
'Tis most true, sir. I heard all; I saw all; I tell all, and I hope you believe all. The sweet Francisco Soranza, the perfumer, is by your rival Jacomo, and your two brothers that must be, when you have married your wife that shall be—

PEDANT
With the grace of Heaven.

BIDET
Disguised so like the drowned Albano, to cross your suit, that by my little honesty 'twas great consolation to me to observe them. "Passion of joy, of hope! O excellent!" cried Andrea. "Passingly!" cried Randolfo. "Unparallel'd!" lisps Jacomo. "Good, good, good!" says Andrea. "Now stut," says Jacomo. "Now stut," says Randolfo; whilst the ravish'd perfumer had like to have water'd the seams of his breeches for extreme pride of their applause.

LAVERDURE

Sest, I'll to Celia, and, maugre the nose of her friends, wed her, bed her; my first son shall be a captain, and his name shall be what it please his godfathers; the second, if he have a face bad enough, a lawyer; the third, a merchant; and the fourth, if he be maim'd, dull-brain'd, or hard-shaped, a scholar; for that's your fashion.

QUADRATUS
Get them; get them, man, first. Now by the wantonness of the night, and I were a wench, I would not ha' thee, wert thou an heir, nay (which is more) a fool.

LAVERDURE
Why, I can rise high: a straight leg, a plump thigh, a full vein, a round cheek; and, when it pleaseth the fertility of my chin to be delivered of a beard, 'twill not wrong my kissing, for my lips are rebels, and stand out.

QUADRATUS
Ho! but there's an old fusty proverb, these great talkers are never good doers.

LAMPATHO
Why, what a babel arrogance is this!
Men will put by the very stock of fate;
They'll thwart the destiny of marriage,
Strive to disturb the sway of Providence:
They'll do it!

QUADRATUS
Come, you'll be snarling now.

LAMPATHO
As if we had free-will in supernatural
Effects, and that our love or hate
Depended not on causes 'bove the reach
Of human stature.

QUADRATUS
I think I shall not lend you forty shillings now.

LAMPATHO
Dirt upon dirt, fear is beneath my shoe.
Dreadless of racks, strappadoes, or the sword—
Maugre informer and sly intelligence,—
I'll stand as confident as Hercules,
And, with a frightless resolution,
Rip up and lance our time's impieties.

SIMPLICIUS
Uds so, peace.

LAMPATHO

Open a bounteous ear, for I'll be free:
Ample as Heaven, give my speech more room;
Let me unbrace my breasts, strip up my sleeves,
Stand like an executioner to vice,
To strike his head off with the keener edge
Of my sharp spirit.

LAVERDURE

Room and good licence: come on! when, when?

LAMPATHO

Now is my fury mounted. Fix your eyes;
Intend your senses; bend your list'ning up;
For I'll make greatness quake; I'll taw the hide
Of thick-skinn'd Hugeness.

LAVERDURE

'Tis most gracious; we'll observe thee calmly.

QUADRATUS

Hang on thy tongue's end. Come on! prithee do.

LAMPATHO

I'll see you hanged first I thank you, sir, I'll none.
This is the strain that chokes the theatres;
That makes them crack with full-stuff'd audience;
This is your humour only in request,
Forsooth to rail; this brings your ears to bed;
This people gape for; for this some do stare.
This some would hear, to crack the author's neck;
This admiration and applause pursues;
Who cannot rail? my humour's changed, 'tis clear:
Pardon, I'll none; I prize my joints more dear.

BIDET

Master, master, I ha' descried the Perfumer in Albano's disguise. Look you! look you! Rare sport! rare sport!

ALBANO

I can contain my impatience no longer. You, Monsieur Cavalier, Saint Dennis,—you, capricious sir, Signior Caranto French Brawl,—you, that must marry Celia Galanto,—is Albano drown'd now? Go wander, avaunt, knight-errant! Celia shall be no cuck-quean,—my heir no beggar,—my plate no pawn,—my land no mortgage,—my wealth no food for thy luxuries,—my house no harbour for thy comrades,—my bed no booty for thy lusts! My anything shall be thy nothing. Go hence! pack, pack! avaunt! caper, caper! aloun, aloun! pass by, pass by! cloak your nose! away! vanish! wander! depart! slink by! away!

LAVERDURE

Hark you, Perfumer. Tell Jacomo, Randolfo, and Andrea, 'twill not do;—look you, say no more, but—'twill not do.

ALBANO
What Perfumer? what Jacomo?

QUADRATUS
Nay, assure thee, honest Perfumer, good Francisco, we know all, man. Go home to thy civet box; look to the profit, commodity, or emolument of thy musk-cat's tail: go, clap on your round cap—my "what do you lack," sir,—for i'faith, good rogue, all's descried!

ALBANO
What Perfumer? what musk-cat? what Francisco? What do you lack? Is't not enough that you kiss'd my wife?

LAVERDURE
Enough.

ALBANO
Ay, enough! and may be, I fear me, too much; but you must flout me,—deride me,—scoff me,—keep out,—touch not my porch;—as for my wife!—

LAVERDURE
Stir to the door: dare to disturb the match, And by the—

ALBANO
My sword! menace Albano 'fore his own doors!

LAVERDURE
No, not Albano, but Francisco: thus, Perfumer, I'll make you stink if you stir a—For the rest: well, via, via!

[Exeunt **ALL** but **ALBANO**, **SLIP**, **SIMPLICIUS**, and **HOLOFERNES**.

ALBANO
Jesu, Jesu! what intends this? ha!

SIMPLICIUS
O God, sir! you lie as open to my understanding as a courtezan. I know you as well—

ALBANO
Somebody knows me yet: praise Heaven, somebody knows me yet!

SIMPLICIUS
Why, look you, sir: I ha' paid for my knowing of men and women too, in my days: I know you are Francisco Soranza, the perfumer; ay, maugre Signor Satin, ay—

ALBANO
Do not tempt my patience. Go to; do not—

SIMPLICIUS
I know you dwell in Saint Mark's Lane, at the sign of the Musk Cat, as well—

ALBANO
Fool, or mad, or drunk, no more!

SIMPLICIUS
I know where you were dressed, where you were—

ALBANO
Nay, then, take all!—take all! take all!—

[He bastinadoes **SIMPLICIUS**.

SIMPLICIUS
And I tell not my father; if I make you not lose your office of gutter-master-ship; and you be scavenger next year, well! Come, Holofernes; come, good Holofernes; come, servant.

[Exeunt **SIMPLICIUS** and **HOLOFERNES**.

[Enter **JACOMO**.

ALBANO
Francisco Soranza, and perfumer, and musk-cat, and gutter-master, hay, hay, hay!—go, go, go!—f-f-f-fut!—I'll to the Duke; and I'll so ti-ti-ti-tickle them!

JACOMO
Precious! what means he to go out so soon,
Before the dusk of twilight might deceive
The doubtful priers? What, holla!

ALBANO
Whop! what devil now?

JACOMO
I'll feign I know him not.—
What business 'fore those doors?

ALBANO
What's that to thee?

JACOMO
You come to wrong my friend Sir Laverdure.
Confess, or—

ALBANO
My sword, boy!—s-s-s-s-soul, my sword!

JACOMO
O, my dear rogue, thou art a rare dissembler!

ALBANO
See, see!

[Enter **ANDREA** and **RANDOLFO**.

JACOMO
Francisco, did I not help to clothe thee even now? I would ha' sworn thee, Albano, my good sweet slave.

[Exit **JACOMO**.

ALBANO
See, see! Jesu, Jesu! Impostors! Coney-catchers! Sancta Maria!

RANDOLFO
Look you. He walks; he feigns most excellent.

ANDREA
Accost him first as if you were ignorant
Of the deceit.

RANDOLFO
O, dear Albano! now thrice happy eyes,
To view the hopeless presence of my brother!

ALBANO
Most lovèd kinsman, praise to Heaven, yet
You know Albano. But for yonder slaves—well—

ANDREA
Success could not come on more gracious.

ALBANO
Had not you come, dear brother Andrea,
I think not one would know me. Ulysses' dog
Had quicker sense than my dull countrymen;
Why, none had known me.

RANDOLFO
Doubt you of that? Would I might die,
Had I not known the guile, I would ha' sworn
Thou hadst been Albano, my nimble, coz'ning knave.

ALBANO
Whip, whip! Heaven preserve all! Saint

Mark, Saint Mark!
Brother Andrea, be frantic, prithee be;
Say I am a perfumer—Francisco. Hay, hay!
Is't not some feast-day? You are all rank drunk!
Rats, ra-ra-ra-rats, knights of the be-be-be-bell! be-be-bell!

ANDREA
Go, go! proceed: thou dost it rare. Farewell.

[Exeunt **ANDREA** and **RANDOLFO**.

ALBANO
Farewell? Ha! Is't even so? Boy, who am I?

SLIP
My Lord Albano!

ALBANO
By this breast you lie.
The Samian faith is true, true! I was drown'd;
And now my soul is skipp'd into a perfumer,
A gutter-master.

SLIP
Believe me, sir—

ALBANO
No, no!
I'll believe nothing! no!
The disadvantage of all honest hearts
Is quick credulity. Perfect state-policy
Can cross-bite even sense. The world's turn'd juggler!
Casts mists before our eyes. Hey-pass re-pass!
I'll credit nothing.

SLIP
Good sir!

ALBANO
Hence, ass!
Doth not opinion stamp the current pass
Of each man's value, virtue, quality?
Had I engross'd the choice commodities
Of Heaven's traffic, yet reputed vile,
I am a rascal! O, dear unbelief!
How wealthy dost thou make thy owner's wit!
Thou train of knowledge! what a privilege
Thou givest to thy possessor! anchor'st him

From floating with the tide of vulgar faith;
From being damn'd with multitude's dear unbelief!
I am a perfumer: ay, think'st thou, my blood,
My brothers know not right Albano yet?
Away! 'tis faithless! If Albano's name
Were liable to sense, that I could taste, or touch,
Or see, or feel it, it might 'tice belief;
But since 'tis voice, and air—Come to the Muskcat, boy;
Francisco, that's my name; 'tis right: ay, ay,
What do you lack? what is't you lack? right; that's my cry.

[Exeunt.

SCENE III

A Tavern.

Enter **SLIP** and **NOOSE**; **TRIP**, with the truncheon of a staff torch, and **DOIT** with a pantofle; **BIDET**, **HOLOFERNES** following. The cornets sound.

BIDET
Proclaim our titles!

DOIT
Bosphoros Cormelydon Honorificacuminos Bidet!

HOLOFERNES
I think your majesty's a Welshman; you have a horrible long name.

BIDET
Death or silence! Proceed!

DOIT
Honorificacuminos Bidet, Emperor of Cracks, Prince of Pages, Marquess of Mumchance, and sole Regent over a Bale of False Dice: to all his under-ministers health, crowns, sack, tobacco, and stockings uncrack'd above the shoe.

BIDET
Ourself will give them their charge. Now let me stroke my beard, and I had it, and speak wisely, if I knew how. Most unconscionable, honest little, or little honest, good subjects, inform our person of your several qualities, and of the prejudice that is foisted upon you, that ourself may preview, prevent, and preoccupy the pestilent dangers incident to all your cases.

DOIT
Here is a petition exhibited of the particular grievances of each sort of pages.

BIDET

We will vouchsafe, in this our public session, to peruse them. Pleaseth your excellent wagship to be informed that the division of pages is tripartite (tripartite), or threefold: of pages, some be court-pages, others ordinary gallant pages, and the third apple-squires, basket-bearers, or pages of the placket: with the last we will proceed first. Stand forth, page of the placket, what is your mistress?

SLIP
A kind of puritan.

BIDET
How live you?

SLIP
Miserably, complaining to your crack-ship: though we have light mistresses, we are made the children and servants of darkness. What profane use we are put to, all these gallants more feelingly know than we can lively express; it is to be commiserated, and by your royal insight only to be prevented, that a male monkey and the diminutive of a man should be synonima, and no sense. Though we are the dross of your subjects, yet being a kind of page, let us find your celsitude kind and respective of our time-fortunes and birth's abuse: and so, in the name of our whole tribe of empty basket-bearers, I kiss your little hands.

BIDET
Your case is dangerous, and almost desperate. Stand forth, ordinary gallant's page: what is the nature of your master?

NOOSE
He eats well and right slovenly; and when the dice favour him, goes in good clothes, and scours his pink colour silk stockings; when he hath any money, he bears his crowns; when he hath none, I carry his purse. He cheats well, swears better, but swaggers in a wanton's chamber admirably; he loves his boy and the rump of a cramm'd capon; and this summer hath a passing thrifty humour to bottle ale; as contemptuous as Lucifer, as arrogant as ignorance can make him, as libidinous as Priapus. He keeps me as his adamant, to draw metal after to his lodging: I curl his perriwig, paint his cheeks, perfume his breath; I am his froterer or rubber in a hot-house, the prop of his lies, the bearer of his false dice; and yet for all this, like the Persian louse, that eats biting, and biting eats, so I say sighing, and sighing say, my end is to paste up a si quis. My master's fortunes are forced to cashier me, and so six to one I fall to be a pippin-squire. Hic finis Priami!—this is the end of pickpockets.

BIDET
Stand forth, court-page: thou lookest pale and wan.

TRIP
Most ridiculous Emperor.

BIDET
O, say no more. I know thy miseries;—what betwixt thy lady, her gentlewoman, and thy master's late gaming, thou mayest look pale. I know thy miseries, and I condole thy calamities. Thou art born well, bred ill, but diest worst of all: thy blood most commonly gentle, thy youth ordinarily idle, and thy age too often miserable. When thy first suit is fresh, thy cheeks clear of court-soils, and thy lord fall'n out with his lady, so long may be he'll chuck thee under the chin, call thee good pretty ape, and give thee a

scrap from his own trencher; but after, he never beholds thee but when thou squirest him with a torch to a wanton's sheets, or lights his tobacco-pipe; never useth thee but as his pander; never regardeth thee but as an idle burr that stick'st upon the nap of his fortune; and so, naked thou camest into the world, and naked thou must return.—Whom serve you?

HOLOFERNES
A fool!

BIDET
Thou art my happiest subject: the service of a fool is the only blessed'st slavery that ever put on a chain and a blue coat; they know not what nor for what they give, but so they give 'tis good, so it be good they give; fortunes are ordain'd for fools, as fools are for fortune, to play withal, not to use: hath he taken an oath of allegiance—is he of our brotherhood yet?

HOLOFERNES
Not yet, right venerable Honorificac-cac-cac-cacu-minos Bidet! but as little an infant as I am I will, and with the grace of wit I will deserve it.

BIDET
You must perform a valorous, virtuous, and religious exploit first, in desert of your order.

HOLOFERNES
What is't?

BIDET
Cozen thy master; he is a fool, and was created for men of wit, such as thyself, to make use of.

HOLOFERNES
Such as myself? Nay, faith, for wit, I think, for my age, or so—But on, sir.

BIDET
That thou mayst the easier purge him of superfluous blood, I will describe thy master's constitution. He loves and is beloved of himself, and one more, his dog. There is a company of unbraced, untruss'd rutters in the town, that crinkle in the hams, swearing their flesh is their only living, and when they have any crowns, cry "God a mercy, Mol!" and shrugging, "let the cock-holds pay for't;" intimating that their maintenance flows from the wantonness of merchants' wives, when in troth the plain troth is, the plain and the stand, or the plain stand and deliver, delivers them all their living. These comrades have persuaded thy master that there's no way to redeem his peach-colour satin suit from pawn but by the love of a citizen's wife; he believes it: they flout him, he feeds them; and now 'tis our honest and religious meditation that he feed us, Holofernes Puppi.

HOLOFERNES
Pippo, and shall please you.

BIDET
Pippo, 'tis our will and pleasure thou suit thyself like a merchant's wife; leave the managing of the sequence unto our prudence.

HOLOFERNES

Or unto our Prudence; truly she is a very witty wench, and hath a stammel petticoat with three guards for the nonce; but for your merchant's wife, alas! I am too little, speak too small, go too gingerly: by my troth I fear I shall look too fair.

BIDET

Our majesty dismounteth, and we put off our greatness; and now, my little knaves, I am plain Crack. As I am Bosphoros Carmelydon Honorificacuminos Bidet, I am imperious, honour sparkles in mine eyes; but as I am Crack, I will convey, crossbite, and cheat upon Simplicius. I will feed, satiate, and fill your paunches; replenish, stuff, or furnish your purses: we will laugh when others weep—sing when others sigh—feed when others starve—and be drunk when others are sober. This is my charge at the loose. As you love our brotherhood, avoid true speech, square dice, small liquor, and above all, those two ungentlemanlike protestations of indeed and verily. And so,
Gentle Apollo, touch thy nimble string;
Our scene is done; yet 'fore we cease, we sing.

[The Song, and exeunt.

ACT IV

SCENE I

Albano's house.

Enter **CELIA**, **MELETZA**, **LYZABETTA**, and **LUCIA**.

CELIA
Faith, sister, I long to play with a feather! Prithee, Lucia, bring the shuttlecock.

MELETZA
Out on him, light-pated fantastic! He's like one of our gallants at—

LYZABETTA
I wonder who thou speak'st well of.

MELETZA
Why, of myself; for, by my troth, I know none else will.

CELIA
Sweet sister Meletza, let's sit in judgment a little, faith, of my servant, Monsieur Laverdure.

MELETZA
Troth well, for a servant, but for a husband
[Sighs]
I—

LYZABETTA
Why, why?

MELETZA
Why, he is not a plain fool, nor fair, nor fat, nor rich, rich fool. But he is a knight; his honour will give the passado in the presence to-morrow night; I hope he will deserve. All I can say is as, as the common fiddlers will say in their "God send you well to do."

LYZABETTA
How think'st thou of the amorous Jacomo?

MELETZA
Jacomo? why, on my bare troth—

CELIA
Why bare troth?

MELETZA
Because my troth is like his chin, t'hath no hair on't. God's me! his face looks like the head of a tabour; but trust me he hath a good wit.

LYZABETTA
Who told you so?

MELETZA
One that knows; one that can tell.

CELIA
Who's that?

MELETZA
Himself.

LYZABETTA
Well, wench; thou hadst a servant, one Fabius; what hast thou done with him?

MELETZA
I done with him? Out of him, puppy! By this feather, his beard is directly brick-colour, and perfectly fashion'd like the husk of a chestnut; he kisses with the driest lip. Fie on him!

CELIA
O, but your servant Quadratus, the absolute courtier!

MELETZA
Fie, fie! Speak no more of him: he lives by begging. He is a fine courtier, flatters admirable, kisses "fair madam," smells surpassing sweet; wears and holds up the arras, supports the tapestry, when I pass into the presence, very gracefully; and I assure you—

LUCIA
Madam, here is your shuttlecock.

MELETZA
Sister, is not your waiting-wench rich?

CELIA
Why, sister, why?

MELETZA
Because she can flatter. Prithee call her not: she has twenty-four hours to madam yet. Come, you; you prate: i'faith, I'll toss you from post to pillar!

CELIA
You post and I pillar.

MELETZA
No, no, you are the only post; you must support, prove a wench, and bear; or else all the building of your delight will fall—

CELIA
Down.

LYZABETTA
What, must I stand out?

MELETZA
Ay, by my faith, till you be married.

LYZABETTA
Why do you toss then?

MELETZA
Why, I am wed, wench.

CELIA
Prithee to whom?

MELETZA
To the true husband, right head of a woman—my will, which vows never to marry till I mean to be a fool, a slave, starch cambric ruffs, and make candles; (pur!)—'tis down, serve again, good wench.

LUCIA
By your pleasing cheek, you play well.

MELETZA
Nay, good creature, prithee do not flatter me. I thought 'twas for something you go cased in your velvet scabbard; I warrant these laces were ne'er stitch'd on with true stitch. I have a plain waiting-wench; she

speaks plain, and, faith, she goes plain; she is virtuous, and because she should go like virtue, by the consent of my bounty, she shall never have above two smocks to her back, for that's the fortune of desert, and the main in fashion or reward of merit; (pur)!—just thus do I use my servants. I strive to catch them in my racket, and no sooner caught, but I toss them away: if he fly well and have good feathers, I play with him till he be down, and then my maid serves him to me again: if a slug, and weak-wing'd, if he be down, there let him lie.

CELIA
Good Mell, I wonder how many servants thou hast.

MELETZA
Troth, so do I; let me see—Dupatzo.

LYZABETTA
Dupatzo, which Dupatzo?

MELETZA
Dupatzo, the elder brother, the fool; he that bought the halfpenny riband, wearing it in his ear, swearing 'twas the Duchess of Milan's favour; he into whose head a man may travel ten leagues before he can meet with his eyes. Then there's my chub, my epicure, Quadratus, that rubs his guts, claps his paunch, and cries Rivo! entertaining my ears perpetually with a most strong discourse of the praise of bottle-ale and red herrings. Then there's Simplicius Faber.

LYZABETTA
Why, he is a fool!

MELETZA
True, or else he would ne'er be my servant. Then there's the cape-cloak'd courtier, Baltazar; he wears a double, treble, quadruple ruff, ay, in the summertime. Faith, I ha' servants enow, and I doubt not but by my ordinary pride and extraordinary cunning to get more.—Monsieur Laverdure, with a troop of gallants, is ent'ring.

LYZABETTA
He capers the lascivious blood about Within heart-pants, nor leaps the eye nor lips: Prepare yourselves to kiss, for you must be kiss'd.

MELETZA
By my troth, 'tis a pretty thing to be towards marriage; a pretty loving—Look, where he comes. Ha! ha!

[Enter **LAVERDURE**, **QUADRATUS**, **LAMPATHO**, and **SIMPLICUS**.

LAVERDURE
Good day, sweet love.

MELETZA
Wish her good night, man.

LAVERDURE

Good morrow, sister.

MELETZA
A curtsey to your caper: to-morrow morn I'll call you brother.

LAVERDURE
But much much falls betwixt the cup and lip.

MELETZA
Be not too confident, the knot may slip.

QUADRATUS
Bounty, blessedness, and the spirit of wine attend my mistress.

MELETZA
Thanks, good chub.

SIMPLICIUS
God ye good morrow heartily, mistress; and how do you since last I saw you?

QUADRATUS
God's me, you must not enquire how she does; that's privy counsel. Fie! there's manners indeed!

SIMPLICIUS
Pray you, pardon my incivility. I was somewhat bold with you, but believe me I'll never be so saucy to ask you how do you again as long as I live. La!

MELETZA
Square chub, what sullen black is that?

QUADRATUS
A tassel that hangs at my purse-strings. He dogs me, and I give him scraps, and pay for his ordinary, feed him; he liquors himself in the juice of my bounty; and when he hath suck'd up strength of spirit he squeezeth it in my own face; when I have refined and sharp'd his wits with good food, he cuts my fingers, and breaks jests upon me. I bear them, and beat him; but by this light the dull-ey'd thinks he does well, does very well; and but that he and I are of two faiths—I fill my belly, and he feeds his brain— I could find in my heart to hug him—to hug him.

MELETZA
Prithee, persuade him to assume spirit, and salute us.

QUADRATUS
Lampatho, Lampatho, art out of countenance? For wit's sake, salute these beauties. How doest like them?

LAMPATHO
Uds fut! I can liken them to nothing but great men's great horse upon great days, whose tails are truss'd up in silk and silver.

QUADRATUS

To them, man; salute them.

LAMPATHO

Bless you, fair ladies! God make you all his servants!

MELETZA

God make you all his servants!

QUADRATUS

He is holpen well had need of you; for be it spoken without profanism, he hath more in this train. I fear me you ha' more servants than he: I am sure the devil is an angel of darkness.

LAMPATHO

Ay, but those are angels of light.

QUADRATUS

Light angels; prithee leave them; withdraw a little, and hear a sonnet; prithee hear a sonnet.

LAMPATHO

Made of Albano's widow that was, and Monsieur Laverdure's wife that must be.

QUADRATUS

Come, leave his lips, and command some liquor; if you have no bottle-ale, command some claret wine and borage, for that's my predominate humour; sleek-bellied Bacchus, let's fill thy guts.

LAMPATHO

Nay, hear it, and relish it judiciously.

QUADRATUS

I do relish it most judicially.

[**QUADRATUS** drinks.

LAMPATHO

Adored excellence! delicious, sweet!

QUADRATUS

Delicious, sweet! good, very good!

LAMPATHO

If thou canst taste the purer juice of love.

QUADRATUS

If thou canst taste the purer juice; good still, good still. I do relish it; it tastes sweet.

LAMPATHO

Is not the metaphor good? Is't not well followed?

QUADRATUS
Passing good, very pleasing.

LAMPATHO
Is't not sweet?

QUADRATUS
Let me see't; I'll make it sweet;
I'll soak it in the juice of Helicon.
By'r Lady, passing sweet; good, passing sweet.

LAMPATHO
You wrong my muse.

QUADRATUS
The Irish flux upon thy muse, thy whorish muse.
Here is no place for her loose brothelry.
We will not deal with her. Go! away, away!

LAMPATHO
I'll be revenged.

QUADRATUS
How, prithee? in a play? Come, come, be sociable.
In private severance from society;
Here leaps a vein of blood inflamed with love,
Mounting to pleasure, all addict to mirth;
Thou'lt read a satire or a sonnet now,
Clagging their airy humour with—

LAMPATHO
Lamp-oil, watch-candles, rug-gowns, and small juice,
Thin commons, four o'clock rising,—I renounce you all.
Now may I 'ternally abandon meat,
Rust, fusty, you which most embraced disuse,
You ha' made me an ass; thus shaped my lot,
I am a mere scholar, that is a mere sot.

QUADRATUS
Come, then, Lamp, I'll pour fresh oil into thee;
Apply thy spirit, that it may nimbly turn
Unto the habit, fashion of the age.
I'll make thee man the scholar, enable thy behaviour
Apt for the entertain of any presence.
I'll turn thee gallant: first thou shalt have a mistress:
How is thy spirit raised to yonder beauty?—

She with the sanguine cheek, the dimpled chin;
The pretty amorous smile, that clips her lips
And dallies 'bout her cheek; she with the speaking eye,
That casts out beams as ardent as those flakes
Which singed the world by rash-brain'd Phaethon;
She with the lip;—O lips!—she, for whose sake
A man could find in his heart to inhell himself!
There's more philosophy, more theorems,
More demonstrations, all invincible,
More clear divinity drawn on her cheek,
Than in all volumes' tedious paraphrase
Of musty eld. O, who would staggering doubt
The soul's eternity, seeing it hath
Of heavenly beauty but to case it up!
Who would distrust a supreme existence,
Able to confound, when it can create
Such heaven on earth able to entrance,
Amaze! O, 'tis Providence, not chance!

LAMPATHO
Now, by the front of Jove, methinks her eye
Shoots more spirit in me. O beauty feminine;
How powerful art thou! What deep magic lies
Within the circle of thy speaking eyes!

QUADRATUS
Why, now could I eat thee; thou doest please mine appetite. I can digest thee. God make thee a good fool, and happy, and ignorant, and amorous, and rich, and frail, and a satirist, and an essayist, and sleepy, and proud, and indeed a fool, and then thou shalt be sure of all these. Do but scorn her, she is thine own; accost her carelessly, and her eye promiseth she will be bound to the good abearing.

CELIA
Now, sister Meletza, doest mark their craft; some straggling thoughts transport thy attentiveness from his discourse. Was't Jacomo's or our brother's plot?

LAVERDURE
Both, both, sweet lady; my page heard all: we met the rogue; so like Albano, I beat the rogue.

SIMPLICIUS
Ay, but when you were gone the rogue beat me.

LAVERDURE
Now, take my counsel: listen.

MELETZA
A pretty youth; a pretty well-shaped youth: a good leg, a very good eye, a sweet ingenious face, and I warrant a good wit; nay, which is more, if he be poor, I assure my soul he is chaste and honest; good faith, I fancy I fancy him: ay, and I may chance;—well, I'll think the rest.

QUADRATUS

I say, be careless still: court her without compliment; take spirit.

LAVERDURE

Were' not a pleasing jest for me to clothe
Another rascal like Albano, say,
And rumour him return'd, without all deceit?
Would not beget errors most ridiculous?

QUADRATUS

Meletza, bella, bellezza! Madonna, bella, bella, gentelezza! prithee kiss this initiated gallant.

MELETZA

How would it please you I should respect ye?

LAMPATHO

As anything, What You Will, as nothing.

MELETZA

As nothing! How will you value my love?

LAMPATHO

Why, just as you respect me—as nothing; for out of nothing, nothing is bred: so nothing shall not beget anything, anything bring nothing, nothing bring anything, anything and nothing shall be What You Will; my speech mounting to the value of myself, which is—

MELETZA

What, sweet—

LAMPATHO

Your nothing, light as yourself, senseless as your sex, and just as you would ha' me—nothing.

MELETZA

Your wit skips a morisco; but, by the brightest spangle of my tire, I vouchsafe you entire unaffected favour.
Wear this, gentle spirit, be not proud;
Believe it, youth, slow speech swift love doth often shroud.

LAMPATHO

My soul's entranced; your favour doth transport
My sense past sense, by your adorèd graces;
I doat, am rapt!

MELETZA

Nay, if you fall to passion and past sense,
My breast's no harbour for your love. Go, pack! hence!

QUADRATUS
Uds fut! thou gull! thou inky scholar! Ha, thou whoreson fop!
Wilt not thou clap into our fashion'd gallantry?
Couldst not be proud and scornful, loose and vain?
God's my heart's object! what a plague is this?
My soul's entranced! Fut! couldst not clip and kiss?
My soul's entranced! ten thousand crowns at least
Lost, lost. My soul's entranced! Love's life, O beast!

ALBANO [Without]
Celia, open; open, Celia: I would enter: open, Celia!

FRANCISCO [Without]
Celia, open; open, Celia: I would enter: open, Celia!

ALBANO [Without]
What, Celia, let in thy husband, Albano: what, Celia!

FRANCISCO [Without]
What, Celia, let in thy husband, Albano: what, Celia!

ALBANO [Without]
Uds f-f-f-fut! let Albano enter.

FRANCISCO [Without]
Uds f-f-f-fut! let Albano enter.

CELIA
Sweet breast, you ha' play'd the wag, i'faith!

LAVERDURE
Believe it, sweet, not I.

MELETZA
Come, you have attired some fiddler like Albano, to fright the perfumer; there's the jest.

[Enter **RANDOLFO**, **ANDREA**, and **JACOMO**.

RANDOLFO
Good fortunes to our sister.

MELETZA
And a speedy marriage.

ANDREA
Then we must wish her no good fortunes.

JACOMO

For shame! for shame! Straight dear your house; sweep out this dust; fling out this trash; return to modesty. Your husband! I say, your husband Albano, that was supposed drown'd, is return'd,—ay, and at the door!

CELIA
Ha, ha! My husband! Ha, ha!

ANDREA
Laugh you? Shameless! Laugh you?

CELIA
Come, come, your plot's discover'd. Good faith, kinsmen, I am no scold. To shape a perfumer like my husband! O sweet jest!

JACOMO
Lost hopes! all known.

CELIA
For penance of your fault, will you maintain a jest now? My love hath tired some fiddler like Albano, like the Perfumer.

LAVERDURE
Not I: by blessedness, not I.

MELETZA
Come, 'tis true. Do but support the jest, and you shall surfeit with laughter.

JACOMO
Faith, we condescend; 'twill not be cross'd, I see.
Marriage and hanging go by destiny.

ALBANO [Without]
B-b-b-bar out Albano! O adulterous, impudent!

FRANCISCO [Without]
B-b-b-bar out Albano! O thou matchless g-g-g-giglet!

QUADRATUS
Let them in! Let them in! Now, now, now! Observe, observe! Look, look, look!

[Enter **ALBANO** and **FRANCISCO**.

JACOMO
That same's a fiddler, shaped like thee. Fear nought; be confident: thou shalt know the jest hereafter: be confident; fear nought; blush not; stand firm.

ALBANO

Now, brothers; now, gallants; now, sisters; now call me a perfumer, a gutter-master. Bar me my house; beat me,—baffle me,—scoff me,—deride me! Ha, that I were a young man again! By the mass, I would ha' you all by the ears, by the mass, law! I am Francisco Soranza! am I not, giglet, strumpet, cutters, swaggerers, brothel-haunters? I am Francisco! O God! O slaves! O dogs, dogs, curs!

JACOMO
No, sir; pray you, pardon us; we confess you are not Francisco, nor a perfumer, but even—

ALBANO
But even Albano.

JACOMO
But even a fiddler,—a minikin-tickler,—a pumpum!

FRANCISCO
A scraper, scraper!
Art not asham'd, before Albano's face,
To clip his spouse? O shameless, impudent!

JACOMO
Well said, perfumer.

ALBANO
A fiddler,—a scraper,—a minikin-tickler,—a pum, a pum!—even now a perfumer,—now a fiddler!—I will be even What You Will. Do, do, do, k-k-k-kiss my wife be-be-be-be-fore—

QUADRATUS
Why, wouldst have him kiss her behind?

ALBANO
Before my own f-f-f-face!

JACOMO
Well done, fiddler!

ALBANO
I'll f-f-fiddle ye!

FRANCISCO
Dost f-f-flout me?

ALBANO
Dost m-m-m-mock me?

FRANCISCO
I'll to the duke. I'll p-p-p-paste up infamies on every post.

JACOMO

'Twas rarely, rarely done. Away, away!

[Exit **FRANCISCO**.

ALBANO
I'll f-f-follow, though I st-st-st-stut; I'll stumble to the duke: in p-p-plain language, I pray you use my wife well. Good faith, she was a kind soul, and an honest woman once: I was her husband, and was called Albano, before I was drown'd; but now, after my resurrection, I am I know not what; indeed, brothers, and indeed, sisters, and indeed, wife, I am What You Will. Doest thou laugh? dost thou ge-ge-ge-gern? A p-p-p-perfumer,—a fiddler, a—Diabolo, matre de Dios,—I'll f-f-f-firk you, by the Lord, now, now I will!

[Exit **ALBANO**.

QUADRATUS
Ha, ha! 'tis a good rogue, a good rogue!

LAVERDURE
A good rogue! Ha! I know him not.

CELIA
No, good sweet love. Come, come, dissemble not.

LAVERDURE
Nay, if you dread nothing, happy be my lot.
Come, via, sest; come, fair cheeks; come, let's dance:
The sweets of love is amorous dalliance.

CELIA
All friends, all happy friends, my veins are light.

LYZABETTA
Thy prayers are now, God send it quickly night!

MELETZA
And then come morning.

LYZABETTA
Ay, that's the hopeful day.

MELETZA
Ay, there thou hitt'st it.

QUADRATUS
Pray God he hit it

LAVERDURE
Play!

[The Dance.

JACOMO
They say there's revels and a play at court.

LAVERDURE
A play to-night?

QUADRATUS
Ay, 'tis this gallant's wit.

JACOMO
Is't good? Is't good?

LAMPATHO
I fear 'twill hardly hit.

QUADRATUS
I like thy fear well; 'twill have better chance;
There's nought more hateful than rank ignorance.

CELIA
Come, gallants, the table's spread; will you to dinner?

QUADRATUS
Yes; first a main at dice, and then we'll eat.

SIMPLICIUS
Truly the best wits have the badd'st fortune at dice still.

QUADRATUS
Who'll play? who'll play?

SIMPLICIUS
Not I; in truth I have still exceeding bad fortune at dice.

CELIA
Come, shall we in? In faith thou art sudden sad.
Doest fear the shadow of my long-dead lord?

LAVERDURE
Shadow! Ha! I cannot tell.
Time trieth all things: well, well, well!

QUADRATUS
Would I were Time, then. I thought 'twas for something that the old fornicator was bald behind. Go; pass on, pass on.

[Exeunt.

Albano's house; a Street; the Duke's palace.

The curtains are drawn by a **PAGE**, and **CELIA** and **LAVERDURE**, **QUADRATUS** and **LYZABETTA**, **LAMPATHO** and **MELETZA**, **SIMPLICIUS** and **LUCIA**, displayed, sitting at dinner. The song is sung, during which a **PAGE** whispers with **SIMPLICIUS**.

QUADRATUS
Feed, and be fat, my fair Calipolis.
Rivo, here's good juice, fresh borage, boy!

LAMPATHO
I commend, commend myself to ye, lady.

MELETZA
In troth, sir, you dwell far from neighbours, that are enforced to commend yourself.

QUADRATUS
Why, Simplicius, whither now, man? for good fashion's sake, stir not; sit still, sit still.

SIMPLICIUS
I must needs rise; much good do it you.

QUADRATUS
Doest thou think thy rising will do them much good? Sit still; sit still; carve me of that, good Meletza. Fill, Bacchus, fill!

SIMPLICIUS
I must needs be gone; and you'll come to my chamber to-morrow morning, I send you a hundred crowns.

QUADRATUS
In the name of prosperity, what tide of happiness so suddenly flow'd upon thee?

SIMPLICIUS
I'll keep a horse and four boys, with grace of fortune now.

QUADRATUS
Now, then, i'faith, get up and ride.

SIMPLICIUS

And I do not, I'll thwack a jerkin till he groan again with gold lace. Let me see; what should I desire of God? Marry, a cloak, lined with rich taffeta; white satin suit; and my gilt rapier from pawn: nay, she shall give me a chain of pearl, that shall pay for all. Good-bye, good signior; good-bye, good signior.

QUADRATUS
Why, now, thou speaketh in the most embraced fashion that our time hugs; no sooner a good fortune or a fresh suit falls upon a fellow that would ha' been gull'd to ha' shoved into your society, but, and he meet you, he fronts you with a faint eye, throws a squint glance over a wried shoulder, and cries 'twixt the teeth, as very parsimonious of breath, "Good-bye, good signior; good-bye, good signior." Death, I will search the lifeblood of your hopes.

SIMPLICIUS
And a fresh pearl-colour silk stocking—O ay, ay, ay, ay, I'll go to the half-crown ordinary every meal; I'll have my ivory box of tobacco; I'll converse with none but counts and courtiers. Now,—good-bye, good signior,—a pair of massy silver spurs, too, a hatch short sword, and then your embroider'd hanger; and, good signior—

QUADRATUS
Shut the windows, darken the room, fetch whips; the fellow is mad: he raves, he raves,—talks idly,—lunatic: who procures thy—

SIMPLICIUS
One that has ate fat capon, suck'd the boil'd chicken, and let out his wit with the fool of bounty, one Fabius. I'll scorn him; he goes upon Fridays in black satin.

QUADRATUS
Fabius! By this light, a cogging cheater: he lives on love of merchants' wives; he stands on the base of mains; he furnisheth your ordinary, for which he feeds scot-free; keeps fair gold in his purse, to put on upon mains, by which he lives, and keeps a fair boy at his heels: he is damn'd Fabius.

SIMPLICIUS
He is a fine man, law, and has a good wit; for when he list he can go in black satin, ay, and in a cloak lined with unshorn velvet.

QUADRATUS
By the salvation of humanity, he's more pestilent than the plague of lice that fell upon Egypt; thou hast been knave if thou credit it; thou art an ass if thou follow it; and shalt be a perpetual idiot if thou pursue it: renounce the world, the flesh, the devil, and thy trust in men's wives, for they will double with thee: and so I betake myself to the sucking of the juice capon, my ingle bottle-ale, and his gentleman usher, that squirers him, red herring. A fool I found thee and a fool I leave thee; bear record, Heaven, 'tis against the providence of my speech. Good-bye, good signior.

[Exit.

[Enter **SLIP**, **NOUS**, **DOIT**, and **BIDET**.

SIMPLICIUS

Ha, ha, ha! Good-bye, good signior! What a fool 'tis! Ha, ha, what an ass 'tis! Save you, young gentlemen, is she coming? Will she meet me? Shall's encounter? Ha?

BIDET

You were not lapt in your mother's smock: you ha' not a good cheek, an enticing eye, a smooth skin, a well-shaped leg, a fair hand: you cannot bring a wench into a fool's paradise for you.

SIMPLICIUS

Not I, by this garter. I am a fool, a very ninny, I! How call you her? How call you her?

BIDET

Call her? You rise on your right side to-day, marry. Call her? her name is Mistress Perpetuana: she is not very fair, nor goes extraordinary gay.

SIMPLICIUS

She has a good skin?

BIDET

A good skin? She is wealthy; her husband's a fool: she'll make you; she wears the breeches: she'll make you—

SIMPLICIUS

I'll keep two men, and they shall be tailors; they shall make suits continually, and those shall be cloth of silver.

BIDET

You may go in beaten precious stones every day. Marry, I must acquaint you with some observances, which you must pursue most religiously. She has a fool; a natural fool waits on her, that is indeed her pander; to him, at the first, you must be bounteous; whatsoe'er he craves,—be it your hat, cloak, rapier, purse, or such trifle,—give't, give't; the night will pay all; and to draw all suspect from pursuing her love for base gain sake.

SIMPLICIUS

Give't? by this light, I'll give't, were't—Gain! I care not for her chain of pearl, only her love: gain! The first thing her bounty shall fetch is my blush-colour satin suit from pawn: gain!

BIDET

When you hear one wind a cornet, she is coming down Saint Mark's Street: prepare your speech, suck your lips, lighten your spirits, fresh your blood, sleek your cheeks, for now thou shalt be made for ever (a perpetual and eternal gull).

[Exit **BIDET**.

SIMPLICIUS

I shall so ravish her with my courtship; I have such variety of discourse, such copy of phrase to begin, as this:—Sweet lady, Ulysses' dog, after his master's ten years' travel—I shall so tickle her: or thus,—Pure beauty, there is a stone—

SLIP
Two stones, man.

SIMPLICIUS
Call'd—'tis no matter what. I ha' the eloquence; I am not to seek, I warrant you.

[The cornet is winded. Enter **PIPPO**, **BIDET**; **PIPPO** attired like a merchant's wife, and **BIDET** like a fool.

Sweet lady, Ulysses' dog, there's a stone called—O Lord! what shall I say?

SLIP
Is all your eloquence come to this?

SIMPLICIUS
The glorious radiant of your glimmering eyes, your glittering beauties blind my wit, and dazzle my—

PIPPO
I'll put on my mask, and please you; pray you, wink, pray you.

BIDET
O fine man! my mistress loves you best. I dreamt you ga' me this sword and dagger. I love your hat and feather, O—

SIMPLICIUS
Do not cry, man; do not cry, man: thou shalt ha' them. Ay, and they were—

BIDET
O, that purse, with all the white pence in it! Fine man! I love you! Give you the fine red pence soon at night? He! I thank you: where's the fool now?

SIMPLICIUS
He has all my money; I have to keep myself, and—

SLIP
Poght!

PIPPO
Sir, the fool shall lead you to my house; the fool shall not. At night I expect you: till then, take this seal of my affection.

QUADRATUS [Within]
What, Simplicius!

SIMPLICIUS
I come, Quadratus. Gentlemen, as yet I can but thank you; but I must be trusted for my ordinary soon at night: or stay, I'll— The fool has unfurnish'd me; but 'twill come again, good bye.

QUADRATUS [Within]

What, ho! Simplicius!

SIMPLICIUS
Good bye, good boys. I come, I come, good bye, good boys.

[Exit.

BIDET
The fool shall wait on thee. Now, do I merit to be yclept, Bosphoros Carmelydon Honorificacuminos Bidet? Who, who has any square dice?

PIPPO
Marry, sir, that have I.

BIDET
Thou shalt lose thy share for it in our purchase.

PIPPO
I pray you now, pray you now.

BIDET
Sooner the whistle of a mariner
Shall sleek the rough curbs of the ocean back.—
Now speak I like myself: thou shalt lose thy share.

[Enter **QUADRATUS**, **LAVERDURE**, and **CELIA**; **SIMPLICIUS**, **MELETZA**, **LYZABETTA**, **LUCIA**, and **LAMPATHO**.

PIPPO
Ha! take all, then. Ha!

QUADRATUS
Without cloak, or hat, or rapier? Fie!

SIMPLICIUS
God's me! Look yonder. Who gave you these things?

BIDET
Mistress Perpetuana's fool.

SIMPLICIUS
Mistress Perpetuana's fool! Ha, ha! there lies a jest. Signor, the fool promised me he would not leave me.

BIDET
I know the fool well. He will stick to you: does not use to forsake any youth that is enamour'd on another man's wife; he strives to keep company with a crimson satin suit continually; he loves to be all one with a critic; a good wit, self-conceited, a hawk-bearer, a dog-keeper, and great with the nobility; he

doats upon a mere scholar, an honest flat fool; but, above all, he is all one with a fellow whose cloak hath a better inside than his outside, and his body richer lined than his brain.

SIMPLICIUS
Uds so! I am cozened.

PIPPO
Pray you, master, pardon me; I must lose my share.

SIMPLICIUS
Give me my purse again.

BIDET
You gave it me, and I'll keep't.

QUADRATUS
Well done, my honest crack, thou shalt be my ingle for't.

LAVERDURE
He shall keep all, maugre thy beardless chin, thy eyes.

SIMPLICIUS
I may go starve till midsummer quarter.

QUADRATUS
Fool! Get thee hence.

PIPPO
I'll to school again, that I will: I left in ass in presenti, and I'll begin in ass in presenti; and so good night, fair gentry.

[Exit **PIPPO**.

QUADRATUS
The triple idiot's coxcomb crown thee,
Bitter epigrams confound thee;
Cuckold be whene'er thou bride thee;
Through every comic scene be drawn;
Never come thy clothes from pawn;
Never may thy shame be sheathed,
Never kiss a wench sweet-breathed.

[Cornets sound.

[Enter as many **PAGES** with torches as you can; **RANDOLFO**, **ANDREA**, **JACOMO**, bare-headed; the **DUKE** with **ATTENDANTS**.

RANDOLFO

Cease! the duke approacheth: 'tis almost night,
For the duke's up: now begins his day.
Come, grace his entrance. Lights! lights! Now 'gins our play.

DUKE

Still these same bawling pipes: sound softer strains!
Slumber our sense: tut! these are vulgar strains.
Cannot your trembling wires throw a chain
Of powerful rapture 'bout our mazèd sense?
Why is our chair thus cushion'd tapestry,
Why is our bed tirèd with wanton sports,
Why are we clothed in glistering attires,
If common bloods can hear, can feel,
Can sit as soft, lie as lascivious,
Strut all as rich as the greatest potentate:—
Soul! and you cannot feast my thristing ears
With aught but what the lip of common birth can taste,
Take all away; your labour's idly waste.
What sport for night?

LAMPATHO

A comedy, entitled Temperance.

DUKE

What sot elects that subject for the court?
What should dame Temperance do here? Away!
The itch on Temperance, your moral play!

QUADRATUS

Duke, prince, royal blood!—thou that hast the best means to be damn'd of any lord in Venice;—thou
great man! let me kiss thy flesh. I am fat, and therefore faithful; I will do that which few of thy subjects
do,—love thee: but I will never do that which all thy subjects do,—flatter thee thy humour's real, good.
A comedy!
No, and thy sense would banquet in delights
Appropriate to the blood of emperors,
Peculiar to the state of majesty,
That none can relish but dilated greatness,
Vouchsafe to view the structure of a scene
That stands on tragic solid passion.
O that's fit traffic to commerce with births,
Strain'd from the mud of base unable brains!
Give them a scene may force their struggling blood
Rise up on tiptoe in attention,
And fill their intellect with pure elixed wit;
O that's for greatness apt, for princes fit!

DUKE

Darest thou then undertake to suit our ears

With such rich vestment?

QUADRATUS
Dare! Yes, my prince, I dare;—nay, more, I will.
And I'll present a subject worth thy soul;—
The honour'd end of Cato Utican.

DUKE
Who'll personate him?

QUADRATUS
Marry, that will I, on sudden, without change.

DUKE
Thou want'st a beard.

QUADRATUS
Tush! a beard ne'er made Cato, though many men's Cato hang only on their chin.
Suppose this floor the city Utica,
The time the night that prolonged Cato's death;
Now being placed 'mong his philosophers,
These first discourse the soul's eternity.

JACOMO
Cato grants that, I am sure, for he was valiant and honest, which an epicure ne'er was, and a coward never will be.

QUADRATUS
Then Cato holds a distinct notion
Of individual actions after death.
This being argued, his resolve maintains
A true magnanimous spirit should give up dirt
To dirt, and with his own flesh dead his flesh,
'Fore chance should force it crouch unto his foe;
To kill one's self, some ay, some hold it no.
O these are points would entice away one's soul
To break indenture of base prenticage,

[Enter **FRANCISCO**.

And run away from 's body in swift thoughts,
To melt in contemplation's luscious sweets!
Now, O my voluptuous duke, I'll feed thy sense
Worth his creation: give me audience.

FRANCISCO
My liege, my royal liege, hear, hear my suit.

QUADRATUS

Now may thy breath ne'er smell sweet as long as thy lungs can pant, for breaking my speech, thou Muscovite! thou stinking perfumer!

[Enter **ALBANO**.

DUKE

Is not this Albano, our sometimes courtier?

FRANCISCO

No, troth, but Francisco, your always perfumer.

ALBANO

Lorenzo Celso, our brave Venice Duke, Albano Belletzo, thy merchant, thy soldier, thy courtier, thy slave, thy anything, thy What thou Wilt, kisseth thy noble blood. Do me right, or else I am canonized a cuckold! canonized a cuckold! I am abused!—I am abused!—my wife's abused!—my clothes abused!—my shape,—my house,—my all,—abused! I am sworn out of myself,—beated out of myself,—baffled,—jeer'd at,—laugh'd at,—barred my own house,—debarr'd my own wife!—whilst others swill my wines,—gormandize my meat, meat,—kiss my wife!—O gods! O gods! O gods! O gods! O gods!

LAVERDURE

Who is't? Who is't?

CELIA

Come, sweet, this is your waggery, i'faith; as if you knew him not.

LAVERDURE

Yes, I fear I do too well: would I could slide away invisible.

DUKE

Assured this is he.

JACOMO

My worthy liege, the jest comes only thus.
Now to stop and cross it with mere like deceit:
All being known, the French knight hath disguised
A fiddler, like Albano too, to fright the perfumer:—this is all.

DUKE

Art sure 'tis true?

MELETZA

'Tis confess'd 'tis right.

ALBANO

Ay, 'tis right, 'tis true; right; I am a fiddler, a fiddler, a fiddler,—uds fut! a fiddler. I'll not believe thee; thou art a woman: and 'tis known, veritas non quærit angulos, truth seeks not to lurk under varthingalls; veritas non quærit angulos; a fiddler?

LAVERDURE
Worthy sir, pardon; and permit me first to confess to yourself,—your deputation dead, hath made my love live, to offend you.

ALBANO
Ay, mock on,—scoff on,—flout on,—do, do, do.

LAVERDURE
Troth, sir, in serious.

ALBANO
Ay, good, good; come hither, Celia.
Burst, breast! rive, heart, asunder! Celia,
Why startest thou back? Seest thou this, Celia?
O me!
How often, with lascivious touch, thy lip
Hath kissed this mark? How oft this much-wrong'd breast
Hath borne the gentle weight of thy soft cheek?

CELIA
O me, my dearest lord,—my sweet, sweet love!

ALBANO
What, a fiddler,—a fiddler? now thy love?
I am sure thou scorn'st it; nay, Celia, I could tell
What, on the night before I went to sea,
And took my leave, with hymeneal rites,
What thou lisped
Into my ear, a fiddler and perfumer now!

ANDREA
And—

RANDOLFO
Dear brother.

JACOMO
Most respected signior;
Believe it, by the sacred end of love,
What much, much wrong hath forced your patience,
Proceeded from most dear affièd love,
Devoted to your house.

ANDREA
Believe it, brother.

JACOMO

Nay, yourself, when you shall hear the occurrences, will say 'tis happy, comical.

RANDOLFO
Assure thee, brother.

ALBANO
Shall I be brave? Shall I be myself now? Love, give me thy love; brothers, give me your breasts; French knight, reach me thy hand; perfumer, thy fist. Duke, I invite thee; love, I forgive thee; Frenchman, I hug thee. I'll know all,—I'll pardon all,—and I'll laugh at all!

[**ALBANO** and his **BROTHERS** talk apart.

QUADRATUS
And I'll curse you all!—O ye ha' interrupt a scene!

DUKE
Quadratus, we will hear these points discuss'd,
With apter and more calm affected hours.

QUADRATUS
Well, good, good.

ALBANO
Was't even so? I'faith, why then, capricious mirth,
Skip light moriscoes in our frolic blood,
Flagg'd veins, sweat, plump with fresh-infusèd joys!
Laughter, pucker our cheeks, make shoulders shog
With chucking lightness! Love, once more thy lips!
For ever clasp our hands, our hearts, our crests!
Thus front, thus eyes, thus cheek, thus all shall meet!
Shall clip, shall hug, shall kiss, my dear, dear sweet!
Duke, wilt thou see me revel? Come, love, dance
Court, gallants, court; suck amorous dalliance!

LAMPATHO
Beauty, your heart!

MELETZA
First, sir, accept my hands:
She leaps too rash that falls in sudden bands.

LAMPATHO
Shall I despair? Never will I love more!

MELETZA
No sea so boundless vast but hath a shore.

QUADRATUS

Why, marry me;
Thou canst have but soft flesh, good blood, sound bones;
And that which fills up all your bracks,—good stones.

LYZABETTA
Stones, trees, and beasts, in love still firmer prove
Than man; I'll none; no hold-fasts in your loves.

LAVERDURE
Since not the mistress,—come on, faith, the maid!

ALBANO
Ten thousand duckets, too, to boot, are laid.

LAVERDURE
Why, then, wind cornets, lead on, jolly lad.

ALBANO
Excuse me, gallants, though my legs lead wrong,
'Tis my first footing; wind out nimble tongue.

DUKE
'Tis well, 'tis well:—how shall we spend this night?

QUADRATUS
Gulp Rhenish wine, my liege; let our paunch rent;
Suck merry jellies; preview, but not prevent,
No mortal can, the miseries of life.

ALBANO
I home invite you all. Come, sweet, sweet wife.
My liege, vouchsafe thy presence.
Drink, till the ground look blue, boy!

QUADRATUS
Live still in springing hopes, still in fresh new joys!—
May your loves happy hit in fair-cheek'd wives,
Your flesh still plump with sapp'd restoratives.
That's all my honest frolic heart can wish.
A fico for the mew and envious pish!
Till night, I wish good food and pleasing day;
But then sound rest. So ends our slight-writ play.

[Exeunt.

John Marston was born to John and Maria Marston née Guarsi, and baptised on October 7th, 1576 at Wardington, Oxfordshire. His father was an eminent lawyer of the Middle Temple who first practiced in London and then became the counsel to Coventry and later its steward.

Marston entered Brasenose College, Oxford in 1592 and earned his BA in 1594. By 1595, he was in London, living in the Middle Temple. His interests were in poetry and play writing, although his father's will of 1599 hopes that he would not further pursue such vanities.

His brief career in literature began with a foray into the then fashionable genres of erotic epyllion and satire; erotic plays for boy actors to be performed before educated young men and members of the inns of court.

In 1598, he published 'The Metamorphosis of Pigmalion's Image and Certaine Satyres', a book of poetry in imitation of, on the one hand, Ovid, and, on the other, the Satires of Juvenal. He also published 'The Scourge of Villanie', in 1598. (these were issued under the pseudonym "W. Kinsayder.") The satire in these books is even more savage and misanthropic than the prevailing norm for other satirists of the era. Marston's style sometimes bends to the point of unintelligibility: he believed that satire should be rough and obscure. Marston seems to have been enraged by Joseph Hall's claim to be the first satirist in English; Hall comes in for some indirect retribution later in one or more of his satires. Some see William Shakespeare's Thersites and Iago, as well as the mad speeches of King Lear as influenced by 'The Scourge of Villanie'.

Marston had, however, arrived on the literary scene as the fad for verse satire was coming under pressure from the authority's censors. Both the Archbishop of Canterbury and the Bishop of London banned 'The Scourge of Villanie' had it publicly burned, along with copies of works by other satirists, on 4th June 1599.

In September 1599, John Marston began to work for the famed Philip Henslowe as a playwright. Marston proved a good match for the private stage where boy players performed racy dramas for an audience of city gallants and young members of the Inns of Court.

'Histriomastix' has been regarded as his first play; performed by either the Children of Paul's or the students of the Middle Temple in around 1599. Its performance kicked off an episode in literary history commonly known as the 'War of the Theatres'; the literary feud between Marston, Jonson and Dekker that took place between 1599 and 1602.

Around 1600, Marston wrote 'Jack Drum's Entertainment' and 'Antonio and Mellida', and in 1601 he wrote 'Antonio's Revenge', a sequel to the latter play; all three were performed by the company at Paul's. In 1601, he contributed poems to Robert Chester's 'Love's Martyr'. For Henslowe, he may have also collaborated with Dekker, Day, and Haughton on 'Lust's Dominion'.

By 1601, he was well known in London literary circles, particularly in his role as enemy to the equally brilliant and difficult Ben Jonson. Jonson, who reported that Marston had accused him of sexual profligacy, satirized Marston as Clove in 'Every Man Out of His Humour', as Crispinus in 'Poetaster', and as Hedon in 'Cynthia's Revels'. Jonson thought Marston a false poet, a vain, careless writer who plagiarised the works of others and whose works were marked by bizarre diction and ugly neologisms. For his part, Marston used Jonson as the complacent, arrogant critic Brabant Senior in 'Jack Drum's

Entertainment' and as the envious, misanthropic playwright and satirist Lampatho Doria in 'What You Will'.

'The Return from Parnassus (II)', an anonymous and satirical play performed at St. John's College, Cambridge in 1601 and 1602, characterised Marston as a poet whose writings see him 'pissing against the world'.

Jonson states that at one point their 'War' boiled over into the physical when he had beaten Marston and taken his pistol. However, the two playwrights were reconciled; Marston wrote a prefatory poem for Jonson's 'Sejanus' in 1605 and dedicated 'The Malcontent' to him.

Beyond this episode Marston's career continued to gather both strength, assets and followers. In 1603, he became a shareholder in the Children of Blackfriars company, at that time known for steadily pushing the boundaries of personal satire, violence, and lewdness on stage. He wrote and produced two plays with the company. The first was 'The Malcontent' in 1603, his most famous play. This work was originally written for the children at Blackfriars and was later taken over by the Kings' Men at the Globe, with additions by John Webster. His second play for the Blackfriars children was 'The Dutch Courtesan', a satire on lust and hypocrisy, in 1604-5.

In 1605, he worked with George Chapman and Ben Jonson on 'Eastward Ho', a satire of popular taste and the vain imaginings of wealth to be found in the colony of Virginia. Chapman and Jonson were arrested for, according to Jonson, a few clauses that offended the Scots, but Marston escaped any imprisonment. Their detainment was brief, and the charges were dropped.

He married Mary Wilkes in 1605, the daughter of the Reverend William Wilkes, one of the chaplains to King James.

In 1606, Marston seems to have had mixed fortunes with the king. At times offending and at others pleasing. In 'Parasitaster, or, The Fawn', he satirized the king specifically. However, in the summer of that year, he put on a production of 'The Dutch Courtesan' for the King of Denmark's visit, with a Latin verse on King James that was presented by hand to the king. Finally, in 1607, he wrote 'The Entertainment at Ashby', a masque for the Earl of Huntingdon.

Marston took the theatre world by surprise when he gave up writing plays in 1609 at the age of thirty-three. He sold his shares in the company of Blackfriars. His departure from the literary scene may have been because of further offence he gave to the king. The king suspended performances at Blackfriars and had Marston imprisoned.

After release he moved into his father-in-law's house to study philosophy. In 1609, he became a reader at the Bodleian library at Oxford. On 24th September he was made a deacon and then a priest on 24th December 1609. In October 1616, Marston was assigned the living of Christchurch, Hampshire.

He died (accounts vary) on either the 24th or 25th June 1634 in London and was buried in the Middle Temple Church.

Tombs at that time were often inscribed with 'Memoriae Sacrum' ('Sacred to the memory') and then the occupants name and a brief account of their achievements. According to Anthony à Wood Marston's tomb stone read 'Oblivioni Sacrum' ('Sacred to Oblivion'), which was probably composed by Marston, and both self-abasing and witty in upturning the tradition.

Marston's reputation through the centuries has varied widely, like that of most of the minor Renaissance dramatists. Both 'The Malcontent' and 'The Dutch Courtesan' remained on stage in altered forms throughout the Restoration.

After the Restoration, Marston's works were largely reduced to literary history. The general resemblance of 'The Malcontent' to 'Hamlet' and Marston's role in the 'War of the Theatres' ensured that his plays would receive some scholarly attention, but they were not performed, nor widely read.

The Romantic movement in English literature unevenly resuscitated Marston's reputation. In his lectures, William Hazlitt praised Marston's genius for satire; however, if the romantic critics were willing to grant Marston's best work a place among the great accomplishments of the age, they remained aware of his inconsistency, what Swinburne would later call his 'uneven and irregular demesne'.

In the twentieth century, however, a few critics were willing to consider Marston as a writer who was very much in control of the world he created. T. S. Eliot saw that this 'irregular demesne' was a part of Marston's world and that "It is ... by giving us the sense of something behind, more real than any of the personages and their action, that Marston establishes himself among the writers of genius".

John Marston – A Concise Bibliography

Plays and production dates

Histriomastix (play), 1599
Antonio and Mellida, London, Paul's theater, 1599–1600.
Jack Drum's Entertainment, London, Paul's theater, 1599/1600.
Antonio's Revenge, London, Paul's theater, 1600.
What You Will, London, Paul's theater, 1601.
The Malcontent, London, Blackfriars Theatre, 1603–1604; Globe Theatre, 1604.
Parasitaster, or The Fawn, London, Blackfriars theater, 1604.
Eastward Ho, by Marston, George Chapman, and Ben Jonson, London, Blackfriars theater, 1604–1605.
The Dutch Courtesan, London, Blackfriars theater, 1605.
The Wonder of Women, or The Tragedy of Sophonisba, London, Blackfriars theater, 1606.
The Spectacle Presented to the Sacred Majesties of Great Britain, and Denmark as They Passed through London, London, 31 July 1606.
The Entertainment of the Dowager-Countess of Darby, Ashby-de-la-Zouch in Leicestershire, 1607.
The Insatiate Countess, by Marston and William Barksted, London, Whitefriars Theatre, c 1608.

Books

The Metamorphosis of Pigmalions Image. And Certaine Satyres.
The Scourge of Villanie. Three Bookes of Satyres (1598; revised and enlarged edition, 1599)
Jacke Drums Entertainment: Or, The Comedie of Pasquill and Katherine (1601)

Loves Martyr: or, Rosalins Complaint, by Marston, Ben Jonson, William Shakespeare, and George Chapman (1601)

The History of Antonio and Mellida (1602)

Antonios Revenge (1602)

The Malcontent (1604)

Eastward Hoe, by Marston, Chapman, and Jonson (1605)

The Dutch Courtezan (1605)

Parasitaster, or The Fawne (1606)

The Wonder of Women, or The Tragedie of Sophonisba (1606)

What You Will (1607)

Histrio-mastix: Or, The Player Whipt (1610)

The Insatiate Countesse, by Marston and William Barksted (1613)

The Workes of Mr. J. Marston (1633); republished as Tragedies and Comedies (1633)

Comedies, Tragi-comedies; & Tragedies, Nonce Collection (1652)

Lust's Dominion, or The Lascivious Queen (probably the same play as The Spanish Moor's Tragedy), by Marston, Thomas Dekker, John Day, and William Haughton (1657)